FLYING

AN INTRODUCTION TO FLIGHT, AIRPLANES, AND AVIATION CAREERS

WALTER J. BOYNE

A SPECTRUM BOOK

PRENTICE-HALL, INC., Englewood Cliffs, New Jersey 07632

Library of Congress Cataloging in Publication Data

Boyne, Walter J   1929-
    Flying, an introduction to flight, airplanes, and
aviation careers.

    (A Spectrum Book)
    Includes index.
    1. Private flying.   I. Title.
TL721.4.B68 1980   629.132'5217   80–13907
ISBN 0-13-322644-1
ISBN 0-13-322636-0 (pbk.)

Photos for the cover and title page
were furnished through the courtesy of
Cessna Aircraft Company.

© 1980 by Prentice-Hall, Inc., Englewood Cliffs, N.J. 07632

A SPECTRUM BOOK
Printed in the United States of America

10 9 8 7 6 5 4 3 2 1

Prentice-Hall International, Inc., London
Prentice-Hall of Australia Pty. Limited, Sydney
Prentice-Hall of Canada, Ltd., Toronto
Prentice-Hall of India Private Limited, New Delhi
Prentice-Hall of Japan, Inc., Tokyo
Prentice-Hall of Southeast Asia Pte. Ltd., Singapore
Whitehall Books Limited, Wellington, New Zealand

Contents

How to Fly: First, Get Your Flight Instructor, 26

How to Make a Perfect Flight, 59

Getting Your Ticket, 78

General Aviation, 97

General Aviation— Where It's At and Where It's Going, 115

Onward and Upward— Time and the Rating Game, 130

The Spice of Flying, 151

The Golden Age of Flight— Mark II, 179

Index, 210

Foreword

Flying is an expansive adventure that's accessible to almost everyone. Today, the attractions of flight are drawing more people into cockpits than ever before.

This book is about those attractions—it explores the thrills and love of flight that so many people feel so profoundly; it describes the freedom that people experience in flight; it realistically defines the steps for getting started as a pilot; and it also traces our aviation legacy, detailing the context for a modern productive encounter with general and sport aviation.

Walt Boyne, a retired Air Force Colonel and current Assistant Director of the National Air and Space Museum, has put together an exciting, energetic invitation to fly. It's designed for beginners, for people who've always stood on the ground watching small planes fly and wondered what might happen if they tried to turn their desires into action.

Walt will introduce you to the airplane, take you up for a vivid, pleasant flight, and explain how the plane flies in language that's easy to understand. Then he'll sit down with you for a briefing on how and why you ought to consider becoming involved in a real flight training program. Finally, he objectively examines potential careers in aviation, along with the vast new recreational uses for the airplane. You'll probably be surprised to see what's waiting for you.

I'm sure you'll find these pages a valuable resource as well as an inspiration. I hope you'll take up flying—it's got so much to offer, and there are so many creative ways to enjoy it or use it.

PAUL H. POBEREZNY, PRESIDENT
Experimental Aircraft Association

Introductory Note

This book is intended for people who have at some time or other thought that they might like to fly, but who have hesitated to begin. It shows you how easily you can move into the aviation scene, and why it is worthwhile for you to do so. It is not a "How to Fly" book, strictly speaking, although it does give insight into the mechanics of flight. Rather, it is a book that tells you why to fly, and where to get the very best information about making flying as safe, easy, and as inexpensive as possible.

Flying is much more than just fun. It is a life-enhancing, fulfilling avocation, and it can be an extraordinarily profitable vocation. You owe it to yourself to find out how you fit in.

Individual chapters try either to give you a sense of flight, as difficult as that is to convey, or to integrate the past, present, and future of those aspects of flight that you are most likely to become part off. At the end of most chapters you will find further references, pointers, and, most important, suggested places where you can go to begin to participate. As a whole, the book covers everything from regulations to the literature of flight, and from how to ensure that you get good flight instruction to whether or not to own your own plane.

It also looks at some hard facts on safety and on cost. The facts here are sometimes startling, if taken out of context. Flying can be terribly expensive, but it can also be approached on a budget basis, where you limit your investment and relate it directly to the benefits you receive. On strictly an investment basis, flying can, for certain people at the right time, be far more profitable than investments in land, stocks, or even a medical education.

I want to thank the many people who have contributed to this book. If I inadvertently leave someone out, please forgive me. My only hope is that all writers receive the same sort of enthusiastic support that aviation writers do from people like: Tom Bliss, Rockwell International; Al Bonadies, New Market Airport; Peter Bowers, Boeing; Dusty Carter, American Aviation Historical Society; Gene Chase, Experimental Aircraft Association; Rick Clark, Air Line Pilots Association; Jack Cox, Experimental Aircraft Association; Nancy Harris, National Air and Space Museum; Thom Hook, Federal Aviation Administration; Fred Johnsen, Echelon; Mike Lavelle, Cessna Aircraft Company; Gary Livak, General Aviation Manufacturer's Association; Don Lopez, National Air and Space Museum; Holly Ludlow, Beech Aircraft Corporation; Birch Matthews, TRW; Philip M. Michel, Cessna Aircraft Company; William Monroe, National Air and Space Museum; Tom Poberezney, EAA; Herb Sawinski, Bendix Avionics Division; Jay Spenser, National Air and Space Museum; and Toni Thomas, National Air and Space Museum.

WALTER J. BOYNE

It's Time to Fly

It's time to fly. You've waited long enough, and you deserve to be satisfied. Let us ease into it. Maybe you'll wind up going solo only a few times and hang it up—but let's at least see what the world of flying is all about and why you should be in it.

The general affluence of our society and especially the pervasive influence of television have changed the character of many pastimes. What used to be sports of kings—horse racing, skiing, scuba diving—have been "Coselled" and "Costeaued" into ordinary events. Only flying remains still a pure adventure for the individual, a private sport that soothes your soul and strokes your ego while making demands upon you that ultimately carry over into every part of your existence.

The most daunting thing about flying is getting started. It seems to be an unfamiliar world, complete with jargon of its own and filled with competent people who might not have time to explain. Not so! It's a place where newcomers are welcomed and where the esoteric quickly becomes the familiar. This book will ease the transition from nonflying to flying by showing you the pleasures you can expect to obtain, the expenses you will run into, where to go to learn, and, perhaps most importantly, the context of flying yesterday, today, and tomorrow.

I think most people are still nonflyers—more than three quarters of a century after Wilbur and Orville got things off the ground—because of the distorted image that film flyers have presented. Buddy Rogers started it in the movie *Wings*, when he did every reprehensible thing possible to his best friend, Dick Arlen. Rogers, the pilot hero, tried to steal Arlen's girl, beat him up, and shot him down—and then kissed him as he lay dying. Thus began the pilot stereotype: a brave but essentially witless hero, more in love with death than with girls or airplanes.

There have been a few exceptions. Jimmy Stewart, in *The Flight of the Phoenix,* comes as close to the portrayal of a real pilot as any, but unfortunately central casting has never come up with Joe Average in the cockpit. And Joe Average does 99 percent of the flying today. Of course, this stereotype in no way acknowledged the presence of women pilots, despite the legendary Amelia Earhart Putnam and the many Jane Averages flying today.

How many times have you looked up from your lawn-mowing to see a little single-engine airplane cross your horizon, its engine puttering comfortably like an old Model A Ford? Often it swings in a wide circle, dipping a wing to salute the proud family below, and then purposefully streaks from sight.

The contrasts are immediate and painful. The airplane is freedom, the lawnmower, slavery. The pilot is capable, alert, and handsome; the gardener is frowsy, unshaven, and tending to a potbelly. Over the horizon there are nymphets, romance, and gusto, while under the rosebushes there are snails and black spotted leaves.

The irony, of course, is that in less than an hour—for the pilot will almost undoubtedly be landing within a few minutes—the pilot will be in his own backyard, weedeater in hand. The difference is that the pilot-turned-gardener is exhilarated and fulfilled. He goes over the flight in intimate detail, congratulating himself where he was smooth and wryly remembering where he goofed.

Gardening is but a colorless backdrop for reviewing the flight, because one of the most entertaining and ennobling aspects of flight is the utter identification of your accomplishment with yourself. When you fly well, only *you* fly well; and often only you know it. When you fly poorly—and you will on occasion—only *you* are responsible. You have no partners to poach on, no caddies to comment, no deck hands to giggle. It's you doing it, and you alone who knows how well.

Flying is far more than the three-dimensional driving that some aircraft manufacturing companies claim it to be. There are no roads, no traffic lights, few traffic jams, and fewer still road-hogs, for the people who fly are notably courteous. Flying is *not* just steering from Point A to Point B; it is an artistic expression of the pilot's care and talent.

An airplane does exactly what you tell it to do. If it moves unerringly from New York to Boston, the crowded highways slipping by below, it does so because you are precise and competent. If you find yourself lost, with no spot on the ground looking like any spot on the map and with big black clouds on the horizon, then you are at fault; the airplane has done only what you have made it do.

(Even being lost can be fun; one of the incidental joys of flying is the impromptu dropping-in on a quiet airport for a cup of coffee and an oh-so-casual inquiry as to your whereabouts.)

Flying quickly shows you how long Americans have been shamelessly pampered by their automobiles. Power steering, power brakes, cruise controls, and mushy suspension systems combined to make driving less than challenging and more than boring. An airplane is totally different: You have to be in command, for it will respond to your slightest wish. You make it fly at certain airspeeds and certain altitudes, and you point its nose along a selected compass course. Yet this aerial precision is far easier than herding a wallowing car along the highway, beset by bumps, tractor trailers, and billboards. One of the really delightful surprises in learning to fly is discovering that the less you do in controlling an aircraft the more readily and precisely it does what you want.

Don't worry about acquiring the necessary attitude of command. Just remember that you share the sky with those who have gone before you and that even the von Richthofens, Rickenbackers, Earharts and Lindberghs all had to learn, just as you do. Remember too that you share the sky also with flying doctors who minister to their practice in Australia's outback, with missionaries who labor in the jungles of Peru, with 83-year-old grandmothers who solo across the Atlantic, with paraplegics who achieve a delicate finesse with strange-looking levers, with rich, handsome, and sometimes grouchy airline pilots, and, best of all, with thousands of average folks. You'll command in flight because you'll learn to do so.

The airplane is not a flying car

When you start flying, the first important thing you'll learn is just how very special a machine an airplane is. When you become familiar with an aircraft, it assumes an almost human identity. Yet even before you are intimate with it, before your hand knows where every switch is, before you can make expert changes in power and trim automatically, you will realize that each aircraft is unique.

We've all seen big used car lots where Mad Man Muntz wants to give away the inventory, but his wife won't let him: With 3,000 cars, vans, campers and RVs on sale, a corps of double-knitted salesmen prowl the lot, which is a lifeless melange of metal, row on row of dull unseeing headlights, dinged fenders, and incipient balloon payments. Contrast this with a big city airport flight line, with almost as many airplanes, but with each one bright, alive, and ready to fly.

The very shapes of cars and airplanes make a difference. The inverted half-pecan-shell profile of automobiles is designed to hug the road, its fat back deflecting air over it while its snarled bottom grapples with the breeze. The airplane is lean-winged and light on its wheels, literally flying in every passing wind even though it may be tethered to the earth. Each plane has a fighter's stance, a ready quiver, poised to leap Nureyev-like into the blue. (If it doesn't, beware, for it's not ready to fly. You'll always see a few of these forlorn orphans at an airport, abandoned by the break-up of a partnership or tied up in a disputed estate. They've faded from proud beauty to shame, and you simply have to avert your eyes.)

Line up a dozen similar airplanes—all Cessna 150s, for example, or all Piper Cherokees, or even all Boeing 747s—and you'll see twelve separate personalities. This statement is not just the customary anthropomorphizing of a love object. It's true. Planes show manners and attitudes at rest that distinguish them from other planes and particularly from other inanimate objects. They live, they wait to fly, they are not creatures of the ground, and they don't complacently assume a common attitude. These personalities develop over time. At factory airfields, where planes are lined up awaiting initial delivery flights to owners, there are great similarities among them. But in the field, in the hands of their pilots, they acquire character, style, and manners. Nor are their personalities limited to the ground; in the air they assume even more defined personalities, becoming comfortable, lovable, or, in a few cases, obnoxious.

Let's pretend that we are on the flight line of a little suburban airport. Among the usual mixture of types, a green and yellow Twin Beech stands over on the back line. If we take a closer look, we can pick out the points of its personality that make it unique. Lots of facts come to mind as we walk toward this Beech Model 18: first built in 1937 . . . in production for thirty-two years . . . longer than any other airplane . . . high performance then and not bad even now . . . 9,000 built . . . a devil to land in a cross wind according to legend . . . for years the Rolls Royce of executive planes. Not so many are around now, because an expensive wing spar modification requirement caused many to be salvaged. Even knowing all this, it

Figure 1-1.   The Famous Twin Beech, the first of the truly efficient executive aircraft and one of the two longest-lived production aircraft in history. The Beech 18 was built for 32 years, a record surpassed only by the Beech Bonanza.
Courtesy: Beech Aircraft Corporation

is obvious that this isn't just one of 9,000 Twin Beeches. This is a Beechcraft D-18, NC 18638, a proud individual.

As we approach, there is a murmuring medley of crackling sounds from the day's heat producing small changes in the sheet metal forming the skin. You can tell some private things about it now, on closer examination. It's been well maintained, for the skin is rubbed glossy with many coats of wax. It's well used, too, for there are stubborn oil stains spread back along the undersurface of the wing. The wing is blown black from engines that have been rebuilt time and again. The big round radial engines glisten with gunmetal sheen, and the tiny little metal fatigue cracks in the cowling are all stop-drilled to prevent their spreading. These are all innocuous signs of age and use and care; the Beech is growing old gracefully.

Crack open the door, and the heady rush of odors, propelled outward by the pressure of the sun-heated air in the cabin, tells us much. There's no faintly sweet garbage smell—the owners have been careful not to let crumbs fall down between the seats; not everyone is so fastidious. Instead there's the warm smell of well-used leather, hydraulic fluid, aviation gasoline, and the hundred other mixtures of flight, all combined into an intoxicating aircraft musk. It smells good.

This airplane is sensual, as most airplanes are; its lines are not abrupt but flow into each other in smooth melding fillets. Step inside the door, and you feel the airplane recognize your weight, hunching down a little bit on its gear. The sound of the ticking clock comes down the narrow aisle, as if it and the rest of the plane were counting the seconds until the next flight. Peer into the cockpit; the old round dials placed in the black crinkle-finish instrument panel contrast with the newer miniaturized radio communication gear.

You can slip into the seat, if you are agile, threading your legs around the throttle quadrant and onto the rudder pedals. The feel of hot leather under you is forgotten as you look down the purposeful

Figure 1-2.   The Beech Bonanza has changed very little in appearance over the years, but it has had many internal improvements and remains the queen of the single-engine fleet.
Courtesy: Beech Aircraft Corporation

array of dials, levers, and buttons. It's all you can do to keep from lifting your fingers to the starter switches, cracking the window open, and calling, "Clear the prop!"

The Twin Beech first greets and then ensnares you; other airplanes will meet you in different ways. A tail dragger like the Piper Cub will seem to smile, knowing that you are of the tricycle gear generation, and that you'll have a hell of a time if you even try to taxi it. A Mooney will seduce you with its slim lines, narrow cockpit, and sharply angled tail. A Bonanza will promise to make a better person of you, just to bring you up to its own patrician standards. Branching out, a rebuilt warbird, say a Candy Tangerine flaked North American P-51, will flood your soul with lust, while a noble glistening Waco biplane, a genuine antique, will call for you to step back with it in time.

You'll see almost any of these at any general aviation airport, those very special places whose flight operations shack is a strange combination of truck stop, fraternity house, and classic P.G. Wodehouse English club. Here you will come to learn the joys of flight.

Airport mores   In the flight operations shack you'll begin to learn the sometimes elaborate code of courtesy and conduct of the flying fraternity and of the informal but usually deadly accurate assessments made of pilots. You'll note that drop-in visitors and students are greeted warmly and get treated beautifully; after all, the airport is a business, and these are potential customers. If you are already a pilot, the mores are rather more complex, and they revolve on how often you fly and your perceived competence.

On your first visit as a pilot, you'll be an outsider looking in, but everyone will be friendly and welcoming. On the second visit, you'll again be greeted warmly, but you'll be under closer scrutiny. Have you been careful? Are you getting along with everyone? Have you been courteous and thoughtful? More to the point, how have you handled your aircraft? What were your landings like?

All this information is mentally filed away, and, after a few more visits, your informal rating will be established. The rating is really based not so much on how well you fly but on how badly you want to fly well. If you are not proficient, it doesn't matter as long as you recognize your limits and make sure you don't exceed them.

If you are eager, courteous, and obviously ready to learn, you'll be treated like a professional. But if you show that you are careless, that you leave your airplane improperly chocked, or fail to turn the magneto switches off after engine shut-down, or run your engine up without knowing what the propeller blast is doing, you'll find the temperature dropping on all sides. Make a habit of any of these discourtesies, and the airport manager will probably have a little private chat with you.

Courtesy breeds courtesy, and, more than anywhere else in the world, an airport is at its best when you need help. The helping hand is a universal aviation tradition going back to the turn-of-the-century air meets. It was firmly reinforced in the golden days of air racing, when racing crews would literally work all night to get a competitor's plane ready, only to see it win the race the next day. If you need help at an airport, it will be there in abundance. Preflighting and forgotten your computer? Need a hand to push your airplane out of the hangar? Just ask, and you'll get more help than you can use.

While helpfulness is fairly uniform at different flight operations, the degree of comfort and luxury varies widely. Some are two-by-four shacks, lined with cheap press-wood ply panels and offering not much more than a table for flight planning. Others are quite luxurious, with completely equipped flight planning rooms, lounge, and perhaps even a bunk where you can rest after a long flight. Often there are two or three "company cars," old but well maintained clunkers kept there for the free use of drop-in cross-country pilots.

It's fun to plan flights from one previously unvisited airport to the next, just to check out the flight operations section, the personnel, and the airport restaurant. Most of the latter are marginal, and some are downright poisonous, but there are enough good ones, where homemade soup and homemade jokes are dispensed, to make the trips worthwhile.

You'll know you've become established as a pilot when you find yourself involved in the joke-making. Pilots' humor usually runs to semi-savage satire, and in most airports the biggest laughs go to the most "in" jokes. Maybe the snooty young doctor, who antagonized a few of the older pilots by buying a brand-new twin-engine Cessna for his first airplane, has been talking a little too much about his general flying proficiency. Nothing's funnier to the folks at flight operations than to watch him taxi out haughtily past the waiting trainers, only to be advised on the radio, for all to hear, that he's left his flight plan, charts, and flashlight on the operations counter.

You won't be spared. The morning that you've done an elaborate preflight, started the engine, made your radio call, and found that you can't taxi because you've forgotten to remove the tie-down ropes won't be forgotten. When you come back an hour later, hoping that your little faux pas was overlooked, you'll probably find the line boy waiting with a suitable axe, marked "For Tie-Down Removal." Afterwards you can count on solicitous inquiries about how low you were planning to fly, or if you need a running start, or whether you wanted to be sure you could find your way back to the parking lot. None of it is very subtle, but it's good-natured, and it means you've arrived.

You, Errol Flynn, and the dawn patrol

Aside from the camaraderie, airport life brings a thousand solitary pleasures and numberless ways to add meaning and fulfillment to life. Imagine, for example, that it's early on a fine June morning and that you're walking up to your waiting Cherokee, ready for your almost-dawn patrol. Moisture glistens on the sleek white wings, and, even though you preflighted the night before, you move around the airplane again, checking every nut, every cotter pin, every safety-wire. You move slowly and deliberately, checking that the fuel tanks are topped off, the sumps drained of water, the oil cap securely fastened, the cowling safely buttoned up.

Then into the cockpit: The tie-down straps are unfastened, you are sure, and you slam the door shut with a solid thunk and lock it. Settle yourself in the left seat, fasten the safety belt, and then bring out the checklist, that detailed listing of what to do and when. You really don't need it, you know the process by heart, but you use it because it's the professional thing to do. The engine starts smoothly, the first sound on the airport, clear and loud in the morning stillness. There's no one in the tower yet, but you turn on the radios anyway, the quiet hum a reassuring factor. Ease out of the parking place, using the same elaborate care you use at noon when the ramp is filled with bustling airplanes. Being careful isn't for the busy times, it's a way of life.

At the end of the runway you go through a meticulous engine run-up, watching every gauge, every light, noticing exactly how the engine responds. Check the sky for traffic. No one is going to be there, but you *always* check the final approach and base leg for traffic, and this morning is no different.

Nobody's coming; taxi out and line up on the runway. Take one last look at the instruments, then bring the throttle smoothly to full power. The Cherokee surges ahead, eager to fly, and your right leg feeds in a little right rudder* to keep it going straight down the runway. As the airspeed builds, you feel the airplane come *alive in your hands*, and just a touch of back pressure on the control column launches you into the dawn.

During the climb, making smooth and accurate turns to keep a check on traffic, you turn the tables of the day. Instead of the sun rising on you, you are rising on the sun, seeing daylight come farther and faster than a groundling, watching shadow changing swiftly as you and the sun go higher. Colors change quickly too, and you see transient shades of rose and green and gray that come only with the dawn, colors that give dull barns new life, change lakes into rainbows, and a refinery into a painted forest.

It's good to be alone in the sky. The aircraft is contendedly doing just what you ask of it, and you know that at the end of an hour you'll have the challenge and the fun of a landing. A little serious airwork, doing clearing turns, a stall series, some turns around a point, S-turns along a road. The hour is gone much too quickly, and it's time to go back. You pick up the disconnected landmarks that chart your way back to the airport. At a horseshoe-shaped lake, you pick up a course of 90° and fly until you cross the railway bridge. A left turn, and you are ready to descend to traffic pattern altitude. The airport suddenly appears on your left as a green square with the two runways, one short and one long, crossing at an angle, a lopsided St. Andrew's cross.

The field is a beehive now. Two airplanes have just taken off, one is lining up, and half a dozen more are taxiing out to the run-up area. You are the only one in a landing pattern so far, but still you check the sky constantly, even as you go through the pre-

---

*At high-power settings, as on takeoff, a single-engine aircraft veers to the left due to the torque effect, the rolling force imposed on the airplane by the engine's turning of the propeller.

landing drill of checking that the fuel tank selector is turned on, the auxiliary fuel pump on, mixture rich, and trim set.

The turn to your final approach is perfect, With the proper altitude setup and the airspeed resting right where it should be. The flaps are down, you are set up. On the end of the runway, the world's toughest audience—a critics row—waits until you land: six planes, six instructors, six students, twelve pairs of eyes and perhaps fifty raucous comments at the ready if you foul up your landing.

It's looking good; the big numbers painted on the end of the runway remain in one spot on your windscreen, just as the books say they should. But there's a little cross wind, and it's drifting you off to the left. Okay, right wing down to kill the drift, a little left rudder pressure to keep you lined up with the runway center line, and you're down over the end of the concrete, beginning your flare, airspeed bleeding off, nose straight, right wing still down into the wind.

There it is—a gentle squeak as first your right tire kisses the runway and then, as speed falls off, another squeak as your left does the same, a perfect cross wind touchdown. It was a great landing. You know your would-be critics have admired it and are now busying themselves in their cockpits, hoping to do as well on their first landing of the day.

Keep back pressure on the control column to keep the nose-wheel off the runway as long as possible, ease it on as your speed slows, and then, very lightly, check your brakes, so that you can turn off at the first intersection.

How very sweet it is to land well, and to land well in front of your peers!

Then it's a luxurious taxi back to the fuel pit, still reveling in the contentment of an early morning patrol that culminates in a lovely sequence of tire squeaks. A perfect way to start a weekend, a perfect memory to keep. It is the real beauty of flying, a glowing sense of self-evaluation and self-accomplishment.

"Easing In"

Flying is the avenue to a thousand good feelings about yourself and the world. It has always been that way, but only lately has flying become generally attainable to the public. Not that flying has suddenly become immensely cheaper—it has not—but it has certainly become relatively cheaper, as we'll see in a later chapter.

A number of questions come immediately to mind when a newcomer thinks about flying. Can you make any money in flying? Yes, enormous amounts if you are skillful and lucky enough to become an airline pilot, for airline salaries are unbelievably, and some say, sinfully high. You can make an adequate living in the military as a pilot—much less than an airline pilot's, but still comfortable. And if you work very hard and are very shrewd, you can make some satisfactory money as a commercial pilot, either flying for corporations or working for a fixed-base operation. We'll look into all these opportunities later and assess the relative probability Joe Average has for success in any of these fields.

For the next few minutes, however, let's forget about the money side of flying, and see how we can find some ways to sample flying inexpensively, to determine if you really want to get involved at all.

The decision to plunge into the field doesn't have to be taken all at once. In fact, it should be approached deliberately and with care. Why not ease into it? Savor the things that are free. See if what you are looking for is the thrill and fulfillment of actually flying, or perhaps just being part of a crowd that likes flying. There is an old joke about the parachutist who hated to jump out of airplanes because it scared him and made him sick. He was asked why he did it, and his ingenuous but honest answer was, "Well, I like to be around people who like to jump out of airplanes." It is entirely possible that you might just like to be part of the crowd that likes to be around airplanes.

Airport bumming The easiest way to get the sense, taste, and smell—and there are lots of good sensations, tastes, and smells—of flying is to do a little airport bumming. It's harder to do nowadays, for airport security is better than it was thirty years ago, when I did my bumming. Yet you'd be surprised at how hospitable airports are if you have the courtesy to drop into the flight operations shack and tell them you'd like to look around.

Plan to spend an afternoon at a small local airport. After you've checked in at the operation's shack, just mosey around and watch the genial, contented groups fooling around with their airplanes. The atmosphere is a lot like a marina, for owning an airplane is like owning a boat—always something to do. But there is another undercurrent at an airport, a low-keyed but unmistakable feeling that flying is still an adventure, worth doing for its own sake, and that the participants all enjoy a common fraternal bond.

After you've wandered down the flight line, noting one family engaged in waxing their Cessna, or a father-and-son team, obviously pleased with themselves, celebrating the son's first solo flight, or a young couple, shy but serious, checking the plane out prior to the flight, you can step into the hangars to browse. Later you'll note that no airplane takes off if there is an airplane on the final approach to the landing, nor will any airplane land if the preceding aircraft has not cleared the runway. Courtesy and common sense prevail.

Watching landings is the most fun. Veteran pilots are easy to spot. Well out on the final approach to the runway, they make precise turns onto the final leg, compensating for any drift from the cross wind as they roll out. They don't make any large power adjustments as they come down the approach. And when they flare, they do it so that they touch down smoothly just past the big white numbers painted on the runway to give its compass heading.

New students are a study in contrast. They either turn onto the final approach much too soon, so that they have to straighten out and fly over to the approach course. Or they delay too long, so that they have to make much too tight a turn to correct back in the opposite direction. The final approach is characterized by undulations above and below the precise glide path that the veteran flies. If high, they come sailing in, a hundred feet over the runway, and majestically glide halfway down the field before the instructor wearily tells them to "take it around." If low, you'll hear the sharp note of power being added as the wary instructor eases the throttle forward to clear all the trees.

In situations like this instructor/pilots really earn their money. They have to decide how long to let the student go before taking over. If too soon, the student never learns. If too long, there might be an accident, and they are totally responsible. This is just one of the stress situations that tend to put instructors a little bit on the serious side.

You'll see a vast variety of landings in just a single afternoon of runway watching, from perfectly sweet touchdowns that justify the name "grease job" to some very hectic Graeco-Roman contests between man and machine. You can learn from every one, whether you are a neophyte or a high-time airline captain.

The magazine scene— the good, the bad, and the indifferent

When it is too dark to watch landings or when the weather is bad, you can pick up an immense amount of lore from the dozen or so aviation publications found on drugstore racks all over the country. *Flying* is, of course, the biggest, oldest, and often the most readable, a slick multi-color producton designed primarily to please the active civil pilot. Slanted heavily towards business aviation, *Flying* sometimes comes off just a little too rich for the average man's taste, with its endless rundowns on the comparative merits of $200,000 executive aircraft. Inevitably, though, it has articles of vital interest to the newcomer in aviation, and it really sets the standard for the general aviation magazine field.

On the industrial side, *Aviation Week and Space Technology* is absolutely without peer. In an amazing job of reporting and editing, *Av Week* keeps you almost ahead of aviation events. It covers all business aspects of flying, and its reporting is so well done that it regularly gets into hot water because of possible security violations. It covers both the national and international scene, and, while expensive, it is vital to the person in business. As a would-be pilot, you can catch up with it at the library, where it is usually on a restricted shelf to prevent pilfering.

For the sport flyer, there are a number of magazines of roughly equal quality, like *Private Pilot*, *Plane and Pilot*, and others, most of which cover items of interest to the less experienced pilot.

One indispensable publication to the would-be aircraft buyer is *Trade-A-Plane,* a (literally) yellow journal that lists hundreds of aircraft for sale, plus every imaginable piece of equipment. It really establishes a market, and if you want to know what a certain type of aircraft is worth, you can usually find a dozen comparable buys in *Trade-A-Plane.*

For history buffs, the United States now offers three good magazines and several atrocious ones, the latter all put out by one notorious publishing house. It can't be named without fear of suit, but it rips off other journals by stealing articles, refuses to pay authors for printed work, and steadfastly refuses to be bothered with petty attention to the details of propriety, authenticity, or even honesty.

The better ones, which I must confess I've been associated with in one way or another as author or contributing editor, are *Wings, Airpower,* and *Aerophile.* The first two are really one magazine with two different names for distribution purposes. They concern themselves with the golden age of flight, with primary emphasis on military aviation history. *Aerophile* has a broader range and goes into more detail of the sort that delights a true buff—serial numbers, first flight dates, squadron markings, and so on.

Yet, Yankee chauvinist though I am, I have to admit that the very best work in aviation history magazines is done in England. Magazines like *Air International, Air Enthusiast, Air Pictorial, Aeroplane Monthly,* and others are simply superb. You can only wonder at the ceaseless flow of quality that issues from their tiny offices.

For the "super" history buff—for the really dedicated historian—there is of course the prestigious American Aviation Historical Society, which puts out a quarterly journal of unsurpassed interest and accuracy.

There is also a booming, seemingly inexhaustible market in aviation books, most of which deal with the history of individual aircraft, companies, or battle campaigns. Books are ever more expensive, and it can bankrupt you if you try to buy everything that comes out. Some, however, are required reading for the student pilot, not because they teach you to fly but because they explain why it is worthwhile to fly. I've listed the ones you ought to read and the ones you ought to have at the end of the appropriate chapters.

After you've bummed the airports and read the literature, you can come one step closer to flying without ever putting a foot in an airplane, if you are willing to get into the immensely satisfying but sometimes nerve-racking world of radio controlled models.

RC—better than CB

Now don't confuse this disciplined sport with the stick-and-paper, rubber-band-powered models of the past. Radio control flying is an art, a science, and a serious business that can be delightful fun, the very next thing to flying yourself.

For many years radio control consisted of little more than a spinoff of radio nuts who were willing to spend enormous amounts of time and energy in building immensely complicated aircraft that were almost doomed to system failures. The expensive radios and especially the support equipment were notoriously unreliable, and, in a literal sense, the sport had a hard time getting off the ground.

About ten years ago there was an equipment revolution. As prices came tumbling down, system reliability soared, so that today you can get by with a cleverly packaged radio control system of radios, airplane, and engine, for as little as $100. And, as in every sport, you can spend virtually as much as you wish, perhaps up to a thousand dollars, to have a sophisticated airplane that drops bombs, opens canopies, and does acrobatics—all at your radio command.

The inexpensive sets usually have only one or two channels, which operate either the model's rudder or rudder and elevator. The expensive sets have up to six channels and operate all three controls—rudder, elevator, and aileron, plus the throttle, brakes, flaps, retractable gear, and so on.

Radio control modeling is really totally different from building ordinary airplane models. Its added advantage is that, if you build your model poorly (as I inevitably do), the radio controls enable you to salvage them by actively correcting for the built-in flight deficiencies. I am a terrible multi-thumbed klutz, whose free-flight models didn't fly well. Yet I have derived countless hours of enjoyment steering my ugly duckling radio-controlled creations around the sky, doing loops and rolls, occasionally making a decent landing, but mostly enjoying overcoming the problems that I built into the model. If you are a good model builder, then radio-controlled flying is even more fun, for you can actively direct it through routines that you may never have the opportunity—or the nerve—to do in real flying.

Curiously, you get only about a 50 percent trade-off on any pilot experience you may have had when flying a radio-controlled model. If you've flown a real plane a bit, you know the effects of the controls, of lift, drag, and thrust, and even of such things as torque, "G" forces, and so on. When the radio control plane is flying away from you, its nose is pointed in the same direction that an airplane's nose is when you are actually flying. You can then do a very easy job of controlling, since your natural control reactions are the proper ones. But turn the model around so that it is coming toward you, and all hell breaks loose. You have to remember to *reverse* the directions of control movement to properly fly the plane. At first it seems impossible and, unless you are lucky, can result in some crashes; but with concentration you can mentally place yourself in the tiny cockpit and make control movements as if you were actually flying. With enough practice, of course, thinking in reverse becomes second nature.

As inexpensive as radio control flying is, you can actually move into two fantastic sports with little or no expense at all, because of the friendly way they are conducted. Also, because these sports are labor-intensive, helping hands are welcomed. Both balloons and sail planes require ground crews and chase crews, and, if you are interested in either sport, you can quickly attach yourself to someone's crew. Let's start with ballooning.

Hot air, warm breeze, and cool beer

The magnificent flight of Ben Abruzzo, Maxie Anderson, and Larry Newman in the Double Eagle II stirred the flying world's soul, and rightfully so. The story of their accomplishment has been told in many articles, films, and television programs. Yet the full measure of their bravery and skill seems to be still not fully realized, primarily because so few people have experienced the pleasures of balloon flying and are unaware of its limitations and its hazards.

The Double Eagle II was, of course, a helium-filled balloon, and not much gas ballooning is done because of the expense involved—about $8,000 per flight. But hot air ballooning is becoming increasingly popular, and you can participate by simply making yourself available for crew duty.

Like many sports, ballooning requires a lot of time to get started and a lot of time to wrap up. It takes a crew of four or five to unpack the balloon, lay it out, hook up the gondola, check the propane burners and other equipment, and then waltz it through the inflation process. Inflation requires the use of an engine driven fan to blow up the balloon somewhat until heated air can be directed into it. Alternatively, balloonists may take hand-held directable propane burners, like those used to remove weeds from a garden path, inside the balloon to direct heat exactly where they want it to go.

In a few minutes the trapped heated air begins to raise the balloon. Soon it is fully inflated, tugging at the gondola and its passengers, who are restrained by the ground crew's grip on the sides of the gondola or on the guidelines. At a signal, the gondola is released and the balloonists are on their way.

Yet the crew's job is not finished; it has just begun.

As the balloon departs, the ground crew quickly buttons up all the gear used for the launch, and packs it into a trailer towed by a husky four-wheel-drive station wagon. The crew then climbs aboard and follows the balloon's wind-driven path, tracking it across field and road.

The balloon drifts with the wind until it reaches a point where the balloonists want—or need—to descend. Once again the ground crew goes into action, trying to grab the gondola when it touches down and keeping it from being dragged by the wind. Usually the bag is quickly deflated and the gondola wrestled to earth. Sometimes, however, there is a little dust-up when the rip cord doesn't spill the hot air from the balloon quite as quickly as desired: Then the wind drives it, the gondola, balloonists, and sometimes the ground crew across the field. Eventually the balloon is subdued, and the ground crew goes through the process of gathering up the balloon, packing it into its container, dragging the gondola back onto its trailer, and so on.

This sometimes chaotic procedure is done with the nicest, most agreeable air of camaraderie imaginable. The balloonist needs the ground crew badly and could be in real danger if these people didn't function correctly. In return, the ground crew members inevitably get to go on rides in the balloon, as the quid pro quo for the services rendered.

And, believe me, a ride in a balloon is worth whatever effort you have put forth as a ground crew member. I got my first ride in Albuquerque, during the 1978 Balloon Fiesta with no less than Ben Abruzzo and Larry Newman as the balloonists. I'd been using

Newman's Cadillac as a chase car (it was stolen shortly afterwards) and waited in a small Albuquerque city park for the beautiful white and orange Raven balloon to come drifting over the trees ringing the five-acre field. Abruzzo let the balloon settle gently into the tree tops to check its speed and then, with a blip of the propane heater, lifted it to drift gently to the ground in a feather-like touchdown. Scores of kindergarten kids came running over. The two ocean-spanning balloonists graciously talked to the kids and signed a few autographs for their teachers. The scene was straight out of the film *The Red Balloon*. Then they flicked the "throttle" of the propane burner on for the lift-off, this time with me aboard.

My more than 5,000 hours of piloting experience had not prepared me for the absolutely unadulterated pleasure of that first ride. We passed over Albuquerque, laid out in squares by its large, straight streets, its multi-colored stucco houses reflected in the dozens of swimming pools. As we drifted, you could hear dogs barking, tires screeching, and a very low murmur of voices. There is no wind in a balloon flight—you *are* the wind—and curiously, rather than feeling detached from the earth, I felt that the earth and the sky were one and that you could just step from the balloon and walk to earth. I didn't, of course—not recommended by the practi-tioners—but the feeling was eerie, quite the opposite of what I had been led to expect. The flight was all too short, about twenty minutes, even though we had some fun-filled moments drifting past the eighteenth-story office window of one of the balloonist's busi-ness partners. Finally settling in over some wires into a vacant lot only a few miles from downtown Albuquerque, I was sold on the sport.

And so will you be if you try it; grab the Yellow Pages and see what sort of balloon activity is going on in your area. Then just go out to the flying field prepared to pitch in and help. It won't be long till you are on your way to your own first flight.

Truly friendly skies

In a similar way, soaring is a labor-intensive sport that requires plenty of ground crew and that has the same gentle, easy-going atmosphere as ballooning. Apparently, many of the people involved are not as interested in soaring as they are in being around people who soar, a phenomenon we discussed earlier.

If you make yourself available, ask questions, and ask permission to help, you'll soon find yourself tugging sailplanes out to the starting line, picking up the tow ropes, holding up wings, and, eventually, following along the path of the sailplane in a crew car. Eventually your efforts will be rewarded with some flights in a sailplane, and you'll be able to form your own opinion as to whether or not you want to pursue the sport.

It is easy to see why people fall in love with soaring, for few sports are so clean, so free from noise, and so dependent on the skill of the individual. Curiously, while it demands a great deal of skill to do well, it is at the same time a very safe sport; you can actually solo at 14 and obtain a pilot certificate at 16, compared to 16 and 17 respectively for powered flying. The reason is that sailplanes operate at relatively low speeds and have extremely effective controls to dissipate the lift of the wings when required. As a result, you are able to maintain a more precise degree of control of the sailplane's flight path than you can that of a powered aircraft's.

With either ballooning or soaring, you have to learn and abide by the Federal Aviation Administration rules, but these are much less complex than those required for powered flight. And with either sport, you can eventually spend as much money on equipment as you like—a competition sailplane may cost $35,000 to $50,000— or you can keep your investment to a minimum, gradually acquiring the hours of time required for a pilot certificate.

But let's assume you are going first for a powered aircraft certificate; after you get that, you can come back and pick up your ballooning and soaring certificates with very little expense. To get into powered flight, you should first learn a little bit about the forces affecting flight, like gravity, lift, thrust, drag, and so on.

Notes on chapter two   Magazines

Aerophile (4014 Belle Grove, San Antonio, Texas 78230). A real buff's magazine with great articles, excellent photos, and details on markings, color, unit histories, and so on.

Aeroplane Monthly (IPC Transport Press, Ltd., Dorset House, Stamford Street, London SE1 9LU, England). An amazing magazine, with diverse, accurate historical coverage; well researched and well written.

Airpower (Sentry Books, 10718 White Oak Avenue, Granada Hills, California 91344). With *Aerophile* and *Wings,* the best U.S. historical magazine; many photos, well researched articles, and good art.

AIR Enthusiast (P.O. Box 16, Bromley, Kent, BR2 7RB, England). A quarterly, but worth the wait; absolutely superb historical coverage by authoritative writers.

Air Pictorial (Seymour Press, Ltd., 334 Brixton Road, London SW9 7AG, England). More of a buff book than other English publications, *Air Pictorial* combines excellent articles with arcane tabulations on individual serial numbers and aircraft movements; first rate.

American Aviation Historical Society Journal (P.O. Box 99, Barden Grove, California 92642). *AAHS* probably did more than any other institution to improve the standards of historical accuracy in aviation writing in the U.S. The journal comes out four times a year with a wide variety of articles on primarily American subjects; a good investment, for the price of back issues goes up continuously.

Aviation Week and Space Technology (McGraw-Hill Building, 1221 Avenue of the Americas, New York, New York 10020). Absolutely indispensable for anyone interested in current aviation happenings. A remarkable magazine, well written, covering the full scope of aviation and space technology. Published weekly, moderately expensive, and worth every penny.

Ballooning (Suite 430, 821 15th Street, N.W., Washington, D.C. 20005). No balloonist or aspirant balloonist can afford to do without this fascinating, colorful magazine; very well done.

Flight International (same as *Aeroplane Monthly*). Another one of those impossibly well-done English aviation magazines. Tends more to the *Aviation Week* side, but it still has great historical material.

Flying (Ziff Davis Publishing Company, One Park Avenue, New York, New York 10016). *Flying* is the oldest, the biggest, and, many say, the best magazine on the market for the private pilot. Very well written, beautifully laid out, with advertisements that are worth the price of the book itself. If you are in aviation, you are bound to read *Flying*.

Model Aviation (815 Fifteenth Street, N.W., Washington, D.C. 20005). Published by the Academy of Model Aeronautics, *Model Aviation* is a good, well-rounded view of the amazingly sophisticated modeling scene. Everything from microfilm lightweights to the fashionable giant-size, quarter-scale radio control models.

Plane & Pilot (606 Wilshire Boulevard, Santa Monica, California 90401). Designed for the general aviation pilot/owner/flight instructor, this magazine fills out some of the gaps that *Flying* magazine leaves for the "ordinary" person.

Private Pilot (8322 Beverly Boulevard, Los Angeles, California 90048). Similar in form and function to *Plane & Pilot*, *Private Pilot* combines interesting stories about people making a living in aviation with pilot reports, articles on technique, and the like; sound.

RC Modeler (120 West Sierra Madre Boulevard, Sierre Madre, California 91024). An excellent magazine dedicated solely to radio control models, primarily aircraft, but including cars and boats; very well done.

Sport Aviation (Experimental Aircraft Association, Hales Corners, Wisconsin 53130). Official publication of the EAA, and a great, beautifully done magazine. Vast variety of articles on home-built aircraft, featuring "how to" on everything from design to metal fabrication and covering the manifold activities of EAA.

Trade-A-Plane (Crossville, Tennessee 38555). A yellow newspaper filled with thousands of advertisements for aircraft, parts, accessories, services, and so on. Fascinating reading, it records the aviation market as it exists in America; excellent trade journal.

Wings (Same as *Airpower*). Really *Airpower* with a different name, *Wings* performs the same function; an excellent publication.

Books

There are literally thousands of excellent aviation books, and one of the great joys of the profession is reading your way through them. We can only touch on a few throughout this book; and these will be recommended primarily for the pleasure to be derived from the reading. "How To" books will be listed at the end of appropriate chapters under "Recommended Reading."

How to Fly:
First, get your
flight instructor . . .

Those Magnificent Men and Their Flying Machines is an all-time great flying movie, for it intersperses really funny scenes (a few of which are slapstick) with lyrically beautiful footage of authentic-looking reproductions of a variety of antique aircraft. One of its amusing subplots was the dogged Teutonic assertion that, "A Cherman offitzer can do anytink," including learning how to fly from a book.

As the channel-ducked *Oberst* proved, you cannot. Flying can only be learned in the air, with a competent flight instructor. But a lot of things can be learned from a book, all of which make your initial cockpit training a lot easier and more productive. Most of these things don't involve rules and regulations, but rather attitudes and perceptions. If you are in the proper frame of mind to receive flight instruction, you will absorb it much more rapidly. Preparatory reading and planning make flight instruction all the easier.

Fear of flight or fear of failure?

A few people are simply afraid of flying, just as some people are afraid of heights or cats or crowded places. There's nothing wrong with this fear, for the solution is amazingly simple: Don't fly. Getting a flying certificate is probably just not worth the confrontations with such indefinable angst. There are too many other fun things to do.

Far more people only *think* they are afraid to learn to fly. Very few people are *actually* afraid only of the challenge. They simply don't understand flying and have not objectively analyzed its hazards.

Flying is not inherently dangerous. Since a qualified pilot flying a well-maintained aircraft in sensible weather is in no special danger, one of the first things you should determine is that you will fly *only* with qualified pilots, in good airplanes, and in suitable weather conditions. If you don't deviate from this simple and obvious rule, you'll never get into trouble.

Many routine events in your life are far more dangerous than any flying you are likely to do. See if at least some of the following risks don't apply to you. Be honest with yourself, and put a check mark by things you've experienced:

1. Driving home from a party where you've had more than two drinks. ( )
2. Driving home on roads where any driver you meet might be totally intoxicated. ( )
3. Working too hard, eating too much, exercising too little. ( )
4. Using a power lawnmower. ( )
5. Making an electrical repair at home. ( )
6. Driving through a yellow stop light at an intersection. ( )
7. Crossing the street before the "Walk" sign comes on. ( )
8. Honking and shaking your fist at a truck driver who has just cut you off in the fast lane. ( )
9. Smoking in bed. ( )
10. Smoking. ( )
11. Weekend athletics, with no sensible exercise program. ( )
12. Lusting after a promotion—or someone else's spouse. ( )
13. Motorcycle riding. ( )
14. Deer hunting. ( )
15. Skateboarding. ( )

Seriously, any of these is much more dangerous than a well-planned, well-conducted flight. If you checked three or more, you are a real devil-may-care type for whom flying should hold few thrills.

Sobering truths   Again, although flying as such is not inherently dangerous, inexperienced "Sunday" flyers can increase the accident rate. Unfortunately, many people who enter flying lose their enthusiasm after a new baby or another car. They begin to stay away from the airfield for longer and longer periods, returning to fly only once a month, or perhaps less. *These people constitute the biggest risk factor in aviation—to themselves, to the people who fly with them, and to the public in general.*

Harsh words, but true: A pilot who flies only 40 to 50 hours a year cannot be proficient even in a relatively small aircraft. Statistics bear out this claim. In general aviation, the accident rate in recent years has been *17 to 34 times as high* as the accident rate for scheduled air carriers, based on accidents per 100,000 hours flown. The fatality ratio per 100,000 hours flown is no better, with the general aviation rate being *24 to 42 times* as high.

These statistics aren't intended to scare you, for that would counter the purpose of the book. Actually, the aspirant flyer has a cheering loophole. *Very few accidents occur in general aviation during the course of training.* There are three reasons for this. First, much of the training is done under the direct guidance of a flight instructor, so there is a built-in safety factor. Second, the student's solo flying is of a prescribed and programmed nature, and it will not normally lead to situations beyond a novice's capability. Finally, during the training period, the student gets a relatively concentrated course, and his or her proficiency is probably higher than it will be for several years.

The real danger period is the time after students receive their private licenses, when they begin building time so that they can get advanced ratings, apply for flying jobs, or just do recreational flying for two or three hours per month. Newly certified pilots, flying at the rate of 40 to 50 hours per year, lose proficiency faster than they gain it; worse, they may not be aware of it and may venture into situations that they can't handle. This hard nugget of truth leads to a fundamental principle underlying the concept of flying being fun, *After you receive your private pilot certificate, you should decide to either pursue flying seriously, either as a career or as a meaningful adjunct to your career, or you should give it up.*

Pursuing flying seriously means flying 100 to 200 hours a year, at a minimum, and maintaining a proficiency by constant training, study, and self-evaluation. If you don't determine to do so, you are a potential contributor to an already critical accident rate. This statement may seem harsh or apparently contradictory in a book dedicated to convince you to try flying. But remember, if you fly only until you have soloed, or even until you get your pilot certificate, and never fly again, you will have made, under safe conditions, one of the best possible investments in your ego. You will have proven to yourself that you could do it for a living if you wanted to, that you have the potential to be an airline or military pilot, but that you made a reasoned choice not to become one. Every flight you make after that, even if it is tourist class in a 747, will be from the viewpoint of an insider. And, if you don't try flying as a student, you'll never know its intoxicating satisfactions. Worse, you might possibly forego getting into aviation as a full-time professional, simply because you never tried.

The best solution, of course, is to get into flying and then fly often enough to be proficient. The best way to do so is to have someone pay you for the privilege.

Flying *is* safe, for those who approach it intelligently and respectfully. Flying is indiscriminately dangerous if you are negligent or indifferent: "Flying, like the sea, is not inherently dangerous, but is terribly unforgiving of any neglect or incapacity."

Flying versus driving

Flying has been described by some soul-less types as "driving in three dimensions." There is a measure of truth in this claim, in that, besides having the capability to go right, left, forward, and backward, you also have the capability to go up or down.

More important than the added dimension, however, is the way the vital force of the machine is applied and how it is steered. In an automobile, the power delivered to the wheels by pressing the accelerator is applied to the earth directly by the rotation of the wheels. The car is propelled forward without any noticeable side-effects as a result of the power's application. In an airplane, the blast of air from the propeller imparts forward motion, but it also has aerodynamic effects upon the vehicle. Similarly, in guiding a car, movement of the steering wheel simply directs the front wheels to move right or left, and the mass of the car dumbly follows. In at least ordinary day-to-day driving, speed does not make much of a difference upon steering; nor does the finesse of the driver. In flying, movement of the control column and rudder pedals affects the flying surfaces (ailerons, elevators, and rudder), which in turn affect airflow, lift, and drag and which also have multiple effects on speed, altitude, and the apparent force of gravity.

The forces of flight

Fortunately, while the physical and mechanical aspects of flight are much more sophisticated than those of driving, they are not difficult to understand and control. Four forces act on an airplane in flight:

1. It has *weight* and is thus affected by the force of gravity. For convenience in diagramming, this force is usually shown as a vector drawn from the airplane's balance point (center of gravity) straight down toward the center of the earth. (Figure 3-1).

2. An airplane also has *drag*, which is resistance to the fluid flow of the air around it. A modern aircraft is carefully designed to minimize drag, which becomes increasingly important as the speed increases. But no matter how sophisticated the designer, every aircraft has drag, and this drag may vary with the attitude of the aircraft and with its configuration.

To offset these two forces, an aircraft is acted upon by two other forces:

3. *Thrust*, delivered from the propeller/powerplant combination, is measured in piston engine aircraft in terms of horsepower and in turbine power aircraft in pounds of thrust.

4. *Lift*, however, is the force that permits the aircraft to fly. It is derived primarily from the effect of the flow of air over the wings. Wings at rest do not generate lift except as the random byproduct of a vagrant breeze. But as the airfoil of the wing passes through the air, a lift is generated and manifested as a force acting in the direction opposite that of gravity, just as thrust acts in an opposite direction to drag.

In a stabilized cruise flight condition (that is, when the aircraft is flying at a constant airspeed and constant altitude), all these

Figure 3-1.   Four forces work on an aircraft.
Source: Flight Instructor, Airplane, Written Test Guide, AC 61-72 (Federal Aviation Administration).

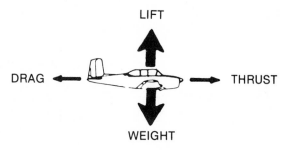

forces cancel each other out. If you change one factor, you disturb the equilibrium, and a change in speed or altitude results.

Suppose you are poking along in your Bonanza at a neat 120-mph indicated airspeed at 4,000 feet, in stable cruising flight. You reach over and extend your landing gear, and what happens? The airplane immediately begins to decelerate, because you've increased the drag factor without changing anything else. You'll soon slow down to an airspeed where thrust and drag are again equal. If you elect to raise the gear, again without changing anything else, the faithful Bonanza will accelerate and in time get right back to your 120-mph indicated airspeed.

In the same flight condition, suppose that you reduce your power by bringing the throttle back a little. The same thing happens—the airplane decelerates until the drag and thrust factors are again equal. If you reapply power, the plane accelerates back to 120 mph.

You can also change the lift factor at will in flight, by changing the attitude of the aircraft or by extending a few degrees of flaps. If you have spoilers, as most sailplanes do, you can reduce lift by extending them into the slipstream.

Increasing the force of gravity is a little more difficult. Generally, changing the force of gravity means changing the weight of the aircraft. Airplanes refueling inflight do this every minute of the day, of course, but any aircraft constantly reduces its weight as it burns off fuel. This decrease in weight, slow as it is, causes the aircraft to depart from its stable state. A large jet, burning fuel at a prodigious rate, follows a climbing flight path to reach its optimum altitude, with the pilot just letting it seek its own level of equilibrium.

Controlling the forces of flight

The entire aircraft is a vehicle for controlling the forces of flight. Some parts of the aircraft act directly on one or more of these forces. Other parts (the cabin heater, for example) are just along for the ride, but they are necessary to make life more convenient, more comfortable, or safer for the flyer. Let's work our way through some terms that are probably familiar to you in the ordinary sense, but that may have a slightly different meaning when viewed in terms of the forces of flight.

Main components   Basically, the main components of an aircraft (Figure 3-2) consist of the:

1. wing,

2. fuselage,

3. empennage,

4. engine/propeller combination, and

5. controls.

Figure 3-2.   Components of an airplane.
Source: Airframe and Powerplant Mechanics, AC 65-15 (Federal Aviation Administration).

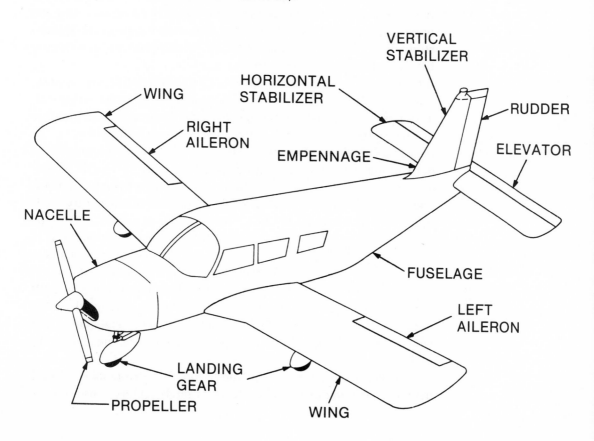

The wing

We all know what a wing looks like. Yet not everyone realizes that it is one of the most sophisticated elements of the aircraft, a component whose style and shape have continuously been altered over the years.

We live in an age of incredibly complex wing designs, created by engineers who have spent thousands of hours of computer time to derive exactly the correct shape for the flight regime intended for the aircraft. The shape of the wing, usually about five or six times as long as it is wide, is derived from a number of compromises. The Concorde's wing, for instance, was designed only after years of studying the benefits of swing-wing versus delta versus its final ogival configuration. Paul MacCready spent thousands of hours on the computer and hundreds of hours with scissors, glue, and mylar to achieve the wing that permitted him to win the Kremer Prize for the first manned power flight in the *Gossamer Condor*. And the wing of the trainer you'll be using was also the result of intense study. It is, like all engineered things, a compromise in this case between desired lift and drag characteristics. In trainers, the need for production ease usually dictates a wing of relatively constantly width (or chord, technically), with smoothly rounded wing tips. The most difficult production problem for modern metal aircraft is achieving the glass-smooth surface necessary to reduce drag.

Like its shape, the area of the wing also has to be carefully determined: Decisions regarding its width (chord), length (span), and curvature (camber) all include not only aerodynamic considerations but also problems of production, interchangeability, visibility from the cockpit, and, not least, visual appearance. Perhaps the most important but least visible of all of these considerations is the choice of airfoils—that is, the camber, the actual curved shape of the wing (Figure 3-3). Yet the airfoil is the very soul of the wing; in combination with the surface finish, it determines how much lift a given wing area and shape generates. The lift generated by the wing directly carries almost all [but not all—the fuselage (body) and empennage (tail) generate some lift] the weight of the aircraft in flight.

Safety is a primary consideration too. As a principal structural member, the wing carries flight loads to safety factors of as much as

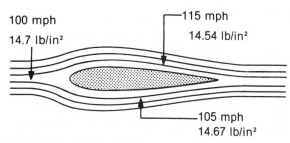

100 mph
14.7 lb/in²

115 mph
14.54 lb/in²

105 mph
14.67 lb/in²

Figure 3-3.   Airflow over a wing section.
The difference in curvature of the upper and lower surfaces of the wing builds up the lift force. Air flowing over the top surface of the wing must reach the trailing edge of the wing in the same amount of time as the air flowing under the wing. To do this, the air passing over the top surface moves at a greater velocity than the air passing below the wing because of the greater distance it must travel along the top surface. This increased velocity, according to Bernoulli's principle, means a corresponding decrease in pressure on the surface. Thus, a pressure differential is created between the upper and lower surfaces of the wing, forcing the wing upward in the direction of the lower pressure.
Source: Airframe and Powerplant Mechanics, AC 65-15 (Federal Aviation Administration).

seven or eight in acrobatic aircraft. In other words, it must support loads up to seven or eight times the weight of the aircraft. As such, it must be stoutly built. It is also stressed to accommodate such additional structures as the landing gear (which, on a hard landing, can impart tremendous stresses to the wing), ailerons, flaps, and so on. Wing structure must also be capable of handling the stress imposed either by high "G" loads during turns or pull-outs or by the ordinary flexing during flight through turbulent air, when the wing acts partially as a shock absorber, smoothing out turbulence by riding with it in a flexible manner.

The fuselage

Like so many aeronautical terms, *fuselage* was originally a French word referring to what is often called the "body" of an aircraft, the area that provides room for the passengers and for the engine (in a single-engine type). It also accommodates the proper mounting and placement of the empennage (or tail).

While the fuselage generates some lift, its design is usually a compromise between carrying capacity, appearance, and the old bugaboo, drag. The designer has to consider such characteristics as visibility from the cockpit, access to the cockpit, access to the power plant, and, as always, the effect of the shape on the airflow (for an obtrusive shape can seriously impair control qualities).

The size of the fuselage is usually determined by internal or aerodynamic requirements—the dimensions of the engine, the need to carry a certain number of passengers, and the distribution of mass to achieve a desirable center of gravity location, the ratio of diameter to length, and so on.

The final design of the fuselage, after all the engineering needs have been met, must also satisfy the demands of the stylists, for it is difficult to sell an ugly airplane, no matter how efficient it is. Many tricks are used to distinguish aircraft or to build in obsolescence. The angle of windscreens is altered slightly, cowlings are modified, spinners are enlarged or reduced, and the rake of the vertical stabilizer is changed. When engineering or economic decisions make real changes impractical, various paint schemes are used to either alter or disguise shapes. There's nothing wrong with any of these cosmetic changes, for the marketplace demands them, but they constitute one of the few areas in aircraft design when anything but pragmatic engineering facts are given a large play.

The empennage

The empennage consists of the vertical and horizontal stabilizers (fixed surfaces at the rear of the aircraft), the rudder, and the elevator. Some aircraft have a stabilator, or a slab "flying tail," instead of the horizontal stabilizer/elevator combination. The Bonanza is famous for its V empennage, which combines the conventional rudder/elevator controls into a single element. The empennage receives the same scrutiny from the designers for weight, lift, and drag as the wing and fuselage do; in addition, they are carefully evaluated for their stability and control factors under all flight conditions.

Engine and propeller combinations

If the wing is the soul of the aircraft, then the power plant is its heart. Together, the engine and propeller must provide not only the motive power (thrust) but also the power for electrical and hydraulic systems of the auxiliary units.

The types of aircraft engines have become relatively standardized in recent years. In the "olden days," as my kids say, a prospective pilot had a choice of liquid- (usually water) or air-cooled enignes among a variety of configurations. There were in-line engines in which cylinders were arrayed like those in a straight six or V-8 automobile engine. There were radials, in which the cylinders were arranged in a fan around the central crankshaft. And there were horizontally opposed types, like the familiar Volkswagen engine, in which the cylinders lay in a flat plane on either side of the crankshaft. Today, for reasons of economy and reliability, most modern light plane engines are air-cooled, opposed types of four or six cylinders. (A few variants are on the scene, especially in the homebuilt arena, where conversions of liquid-cooled automobile engines are getting careful evaluations.)

Aircraft engines—and all aircraft parts in general—are inherently much more expensive than automobile engines of equivalent size. For example, a 150-horsepower Lycoming engine, fully built up for installation, costs about five times as much as the equivalent automobile engine. The best reason for this difference is that a failed automobile engine usually results in a quiet roll to the side of the road, while an engine failure in the air poses more dramatic problems. Consequently, aircraft engines are developed to be extremely reliable, even though they operate for a great percentage of their life at or near 100-percent power—something that an ordinary automobile engine does only in the rarest circumstances.

Because they are so expensive and because you need them so much while flying, pilots tend to baby aircraft engines much more than they do automobile engines. Stringent maintenance requirements are closely followed, as are instructions for starting, warmup, and inflight operation.

The propeller, that silver scimitar on the front of the plane, is another engineering masterpiece. It is carefully chosen for its compatibility with the engine and airframe, and, because it is a wing itself (albeit a rotating one), it is also the product of the same systematic analysis of airfoil, weight, length, and control characteristics. An unforgiving ground hazard, it describes a lethal arc, and, like a loaded gun, it must always be approached and handled with care. An experienced pilot *never* walks through the arc of a propeller of a parked aircraft, even though he or she has personally shut it down and turned the magneto switches off.

The controls

Ailerons. These controls are the small airfoils found on the outboard side of the wing's trailing edge. They are hinged to the wing and operated by the control column's wheel (or more rarely, the stick) in the cockpit. Ailerons are designed to operate differentially; that is, if the control wheel is moved to the right, the right aileron is deflected to the up position, while the left is deflected to the down position. The right aileron, moving up, has the effect of reducing lift on the right wing, while the left (or down) aileron increases lift on its side. The net effect is that the aircraft rolls into a bank about its longitudinal axis (Figure 3-4), thus causing the aircraft to turn.*

Rudder. The rudder is attached to the vertical stabilizer as the aileron is attached to the wing. While the vertical fin is fixed and intended to provide lateral stability in flight, the hinged rudder responds to the movement of the foot-operated rudder pedals. In effect, the rudder controls movement around the vertical axis of the aircraft (Figure 3-4). Oddly enough, the rudder does not *turn* the aircraft in the air as a ship's rudder turns it in the water. Instead it controls the movement of the aircraft's nose and, when turning, provides control forces that supplement and coordinate the movement of the ailerons.

Elevators. The *elevators*, hinged to the rear of the vertical fin, provide part of the longitudinal stability. The elevators are linked

---

*Rolling or banking an aircraft causes lift forces to be divided into vertical and horizontal components. It is that horizontal component, combined with the thrust force, that causes an aircraft to turn along a prescribed path.

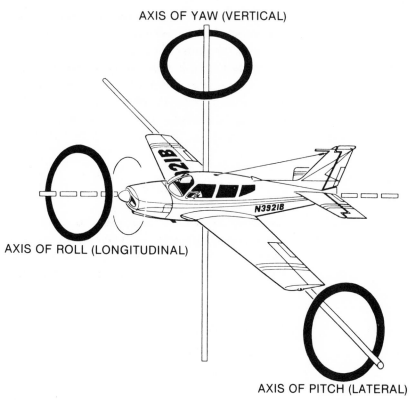

AXIS OF YAW (VERTICAL)

AXIS OF ROLL (LONGITUDINAL)

AXIS OF PITCH (LATERAL)

Figure 3-4.   Yaw, roll, and pitch.
Source: Flight Instructor, Airplane, Written Test Guide, AC 61-72
(Federal Aviation Administration).

to the fore and aft movement of the control column. If you move the control column forward, you lower the elevators and thus cause the nose of the airplane to pitch downward, entering a dive. If you move the control column back, you raise the elevator, causing the nose of the aircraft to pitch upward, entering a climb. Figure 3-4 shows how movement around the lateral axis (pitch) is controlled by the elevators. The nose is raised to increase the wings' angle of attack and to give them more lift; lowering the nose decreases the angle of attack and reduces lift.

These primary control surfaces—ailerons, rudder, and elevators—are almost always used simultaneously for coordinated flight. Perhaps their most unusual characteristic is the very small amount of movement applied to the control column or rudder pedals to obtain the desired aerodynamic effect. In many airplanes, a gentle pressure, no more than a suggestion of movement, is all that is necessary to obtain the desired response. One of your flight instructor's biggest challenges is to convince you that only a slight pressure of the controls is required. Most students tend to overcontrol violently, a perfectly normal reaction in the early stages of flight instruction.

Secondary components

The term "secondary" is applied to components because an aircraft can be created without them. When installed, however, they provide additional utility and efficiency that give the airplane a lot more capability. Secondary components usually include:

1. flaps,
2. the throttle,
3. trim tabs, and
4. various other controls.

The flaps. Flaps are auxiliary controls that permit an aircraft to be designed for higher cruise speeds without loss of takeoff and landing capability. Flaps are always mounted inboard of the ailerons on the trailing edge of the wing. ("Always" is a bad word—there are inevitable exceptions to the rule, but these are very rare, especially in the world of flight trainers.)

Flaps are arranged to lower symmetrically (unlike the opposing operation of ailerons) and usually have only two or three settings, ranging from full up through 10°, 25°, or 40° down. At the lower settings (10°, say) you obtain an increase in both lift and drag, while at the higher settings, you obtain a much larger increase in drag than in lift.

The flap is designed less to permit shorter takeoff and landing runs than it is to permit landings at steeper angles of descent while maintaining a relatively low airspeed. The lowering of flaps provide, in effect, a "low-speed wing" for takeoff and landing, and the retraction of flaps make for a "high-speed wing" for cruising flight.

The throttle. The throttle is not often considered a control, in that it has no direct aerodynamic effect. But since it controls the power from the engine, it enables the pilot to control the speed (and in turn the lift) and sometimes the attitude of the aircraft.

Trim tabs. Most aircraft are designed to be stable in flight at certain power and control settings. *Power settings* are the adjustments made to the propeller and throttle controls, and *control settings* pertain to the manipulation of the rudders, elevators, and ailerons. However, constantly applying the necessary control forces to keep the aircraft at a certain airspeed and altitude could become fatiguing to a pilot. Consequently trim tabs are built into the control surfaces of most aircraft, and the pilot adjusts these to bring the airplane into a stable, unchanging flight condition.

On larger aircraft the trimming devices are (usually, but not always, tabs) mounted on all three sets of controls and adjusted from the cockpit. If, for example, you wish to maintain the same altitude but increase power, you increase the power setting. The natural reaction of the aircraft is to climb. Instead, you apply forward pressure to the control column and, using the elevators, lower the pitch, thereby maintaining the same altitude. When the speed has stabilized at the new figure you want, gently "trim" away the additional forward force you are holding on the control column by adjusting the trim tab. The tab applies aerodynamic forces on the elevator, which relieves you of the necessity of applying pressure to the control column in the cockpit. Although the mechanics are different, basically the same thing happens in an aircraft with a "flying" or slab tail.

Trim tabs are thus very handy. They were, in fact, a revolutionary advance when they were introduced into general use in the years following the first World War. Formerly aircraft had been designed to fly "hands off" only at certain specified speeds and flight conditions; anything else, and the poor pilot had to wrestle continuously with aerodynamic pressures. On a long flight, the pilot would land in a state of exhaustion, still fighting a fractious out-of-trim airplane; no wonder there were so many landing accidents.

Rudder trim is used to offset changes in power, particularly when large changes are made, as in takeoff, or when multi-engine aircraft suffer an engine failure on one side and experience increased power on the other. As in the case of elevator trim, the rudder trim tab is simply adjusted to apply aerodynamic forces to the rudder, relieving the pilot of the need to apply forces to the rudder pedal.

Aileron trim tabs are not as essential as the first two, and many aircraft are manufactured with simple metal tabs, adjustable only on the ground. If an aircraft flies "wing low" because it isn't rigged properly or because it has some unusual drag characteristic (a pylon added on one side, for example), aileron tabs are useful to bring it back into trim.

Other controls. We won't worry about the variety of other controls—spoilers, slats, leading edge devices, and so on. You'll encounter them on the flight line and in the literature, and you'll have plenty of time to get acquainted.

Auxiliary components

Hundreds, even thousands, of aircraft components are "auxiliary" in the sense that they are not necessary to control the forces of flight, although they may be vital to certain other operations. "Auxiliary" doesn't mean "unimportant" in reference to aircraft— just not directly related to the lift, drag, thrust, and gravity considerations. In this context, therefore, we will limit our discussion of such components to the landing gear and the cockpit.

Landing gear

While modern aircraft are almost standardized on the tricycle gear layout, it was not always so. There have been in fact almost as many types of landing gear as varieties of engines or differences in wing configurations. The Wrights actually started off with skids, while Glen Curtiss, very farsightedly, chose a tricycle gear arrangement. During one period, every sort of combination was tried, not so much to land as to prevent the aircraft from turning over. In time, however, engineers became adept enough to use minimal landing gear, two wheels and a tail skid, for they were concerned more about weight and drag than ground-handling characteristics. This "conventional" arrangement, fondly known today as a "tail-dragger," was modified in time to incorporate a tail wheel, brakes, and even a retraction mechanism. In the late 1930s, however, the distinct advantages of the tricycle landing gear became generally known, and by the end of World War II almost all commercial and military aircraft were designed with three wheels.

The tricycle landing gear has many advantages to offset its slight increase in weight. It allows an aircraft to be inherently more stable, vastly improves ground-handling during taxi, takeoff, and landing, and eases the engineer's general problem of distributing weight and locating the landing gear at the points of structural strength. In airliners it made the cabin easier to enter, as anyone who has had to climb uphill in a DC-3 recognizes.

For the beginner, the main benefit is that the tricycle gear makes the airplane much easier to land, so that it takes separate instruction to qualify in a tail wheel type aircraft. The relationship of the main wheels to the airplane's center of gravity makes it much more stable after touchdown, and when the nose wheel comes down, steering the plane on the runway is much easier than steering an automobile.

Before leaving the landing gear, we should comment on its built-in ruggedness. Landing gears are designed to sustain several times the weight of the aircraft, a factor you'll be glad of the first time you stall one several feet above the runway. Yet even though the gear is rugged, the stresses it must absorb make it mandatory that it be inspected carefully before each flight and be well-maintained at all times.

The cockpit

The cockpit is really an assembly of minor components, and on first look it can be pretty intimidating, with its array of dials, gauges, levers, and the like. (See Figure 3-5.) It is really not that complex, however, for everything is positioned in a logical manner relating to the individual item's importance, frequency of use, and relation to other components. Only a few of the dials and switches need to be used at any one time, so you need not continuously integrate all the information presented. Instead, you selectively read the applicable instruments or use the necessary switch as required. Most pilots become so at home in their cockpit—even a 747's—that it becomes as familiar as an office desk.

Figure 3-5.   The cockpit of the Beech Sundowner is well laid out. The instruments and controls are arranged in a logical, easy-to-use pattern.
Courtesy: Beech Aircraft Corporation

The control devices in a cockpit are a little different from an automobile's. Aileron control is accomplished by the right-and-left movement of the wheel, while the elevator is controlled by the fore-and-aft movement of the control column. The rudder is controlled by foot pedals, which also contain the brakes on the upper part, or toe position.

There is a vast difference in how these controls feel on the ground and in the air. On the ground they are lifeless, for without a windstream over them you can move them effortlessly through their full movement. In the air, only the slightest movement is necessary; you can look out on the canopy during a steep turn and see your ailerons only slightly deflected. In addition, when you are flying, you get an immediate attitudinal response from your airplane that imparts a direct feeling to the controls, depending on which maneuver you are doing. Another more pedestrian reason is that the rudder controls perform an additional function on the ground. Besides moving the rudder, they also steer the nose wheel, and with their use you can "lead" your aircraft adroitly around the airfield.

The pedal-mounted brakes are independent, so they can help you make tight turns. It's best to minimize the use of brakes on the ground, however, for they tend to heat up and lose effectiveness if over-used.

In terms of levers and switches, you have the throttle and propeller controls to control power, a master switch, magneto and starter switches (sometimes combined into one switch), as well as levers to control the fuel mixture, cabin air, and heat. Naturally, more sophisticated aircraft offer more varied sometimes more complex controls. You'll become familiar with these quickly and with only a little practice, just as you will with the radio and communication gear.

Let's talk about the basic instruments and controls for a bit, just to give you a little familiarity with them. The instrument panel as a whole can be conveniently broken down into three general sets of instruments: (1) flight, (2) engine, and (3) "all other."

Basic flight instruments

The basic flight instruments include an:

1. airspeed indicator,

2. altimeter,

3. vertical velocity indicator, and

4. various directional instruments.

Airspeed indicator

The only flight instrument directly comparable to an instrument on an automobile dash panel is the airspeed indicator (Figure 3-6), which corresponds roughly to the speedometer. The speedometer receives its information via a cable attached to some part of the automobile that furnishes information on speed over the ground. The airspeed indicator measures the difference between static air (non-moving) pressure and "impact" (moving) air in a fork- or spear-shaped device known as the *pitot tube* (Figure 3-7). When the plane is at rest, there is no difference between static and impact pressure, and the airspeed indicator reads zero. When the plane

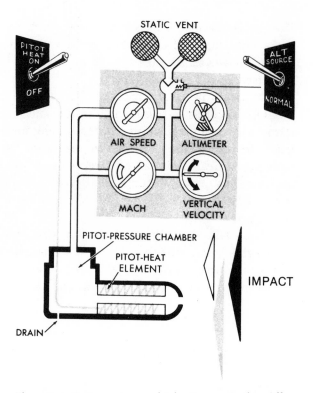

Figure 3-6. The pitot-static system, which measures the difference between impact air and static air, is used by four different instruments: the airspeed indicator, the altimeter, the vertical velocity, and, in high performance aircraft, the Machmeter. The alternate source is for use in the event of icing or other problem to the main system; the pitot heat is to prevent icing.
Source: Air Force Manual 51-37, Instrument Flying.

moves through the air, the impact pressure increases and is registered as airspeed on the indicator.

The most significant difference between an airspeed indicator and an automobile speedometer is that the former measures speed through the air, **not** over the ground. Actually, it measures the impact pressure as an indication of speed, not the aircraft's speed itself. Thus, at the proper power setting, an airspeed indicator indicates the same impact pressure, whether you are flying in still air or in a strong head- or tailwind. Your groundspeed, however, is

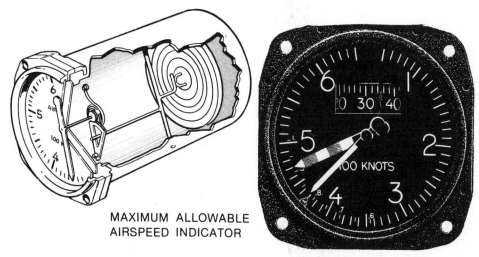

MAXIMUM ALLOWABLE
AIRSPEED INDICATOR

Figure 3-7.   The airspeed indicator.
Source: Air Force Manual 51-37, Instrument Flying.

the exact plus or minus difference of the effect of the wind. For example, your airspeed indicator shows, say, 100 knots, which is actually only a reading of impact pressure. If you were headed directly into a 20-knot wind, your groundspeed would be only 80 knots (100 knots − 20 knots). If you were headed directly away from the wind, your groundspeed would be 120 knots (100 knots + 20 knots).

The altimeter

The altimeter (Figure 3-8) tells you how high you are by measuring the difference in air pressure as you ascend or descend. *In simplest terms, an altimeter is simply a special form of barometer, one that gives its information in terms of feet rather than pressure.* Since convention dictates that all altitude is measured from sea level, all the altimeters of all the airplanes located at a mythical airport situated exactly one mile above sea level would theoretically read 5,280 feet. This is not exactly true, of course, for differences in atmospheric pressure occur as air masses move through the area, and corrections must be made for these differences.

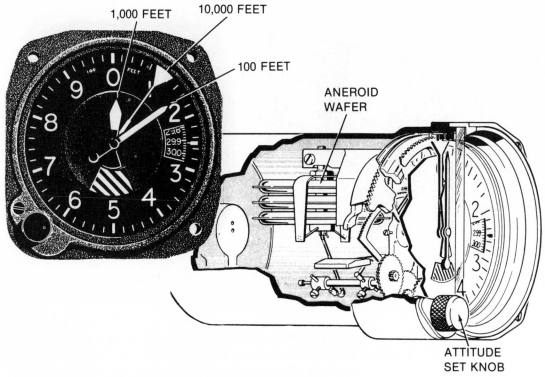

1,000 FEET   10,000 FEET

100 FEET

ANEROID
WAFER

ATTITUDE
SET KNOB

Figure 3-8.   Cutaway view of the altimeter.
Source: Air Force Manual 51-37, Instrument Flying.

It is important to adjust the altimeter, by means of a small manual adjustment knob, for these local variations in air pressure. Information for this adjustment is received from the tower, from the weather office, or en route from flight service stations. Adjustments are made before flight and before landing, for certain, and as often as information is received during a flight.

Vertical velocity indicator

Often called the "rate of climb" instrument, although it measures both climbs and descents, the vertical velocity indicator is also a differential pressure instrument (Figure 3-9). In this case it measures the difference between outside atmospheric pressure and the trap-

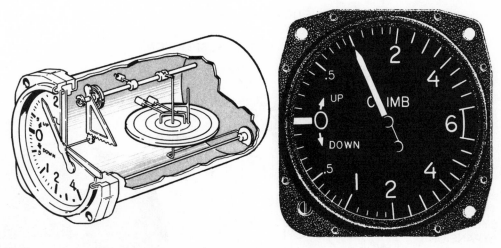

Figure3-9.   Vertical velocity indicator.
Source: Air Force Manual 51-37, Instrument Flying.

ped static pressure within the instrument case. The purpose of the instrument, obviously enough, is to tell you the *rate* at which you are climbing or descending.

The vertical velocity indicator is extremely useful as a supplement to the other flight instruments, but it has a built-in lag in its response that must always be considered. Very useful as a trend instrument, it signals an incipient climb or descent sometimes when you have not picked it up on other instruments.

Directional instruments

The magnetic compass. A mag compass in an airplane performs the same functions that it does on land or in a ship—it provides a guide to magnetic north and a means of holding to other desired courses (Figure 3-10). In an airplane it is subject to certain errors not encountered on the surface—acceleration and deceleration, for example—but there is no essential difference in its use.

Heading indicators. Because the forces of flight sometimes make it difficult to read a freely turning magnetic compass, several forms of heading indicators have been developed (Figure 3-11). Essentially, these instruments use a gyroscope to maintain the

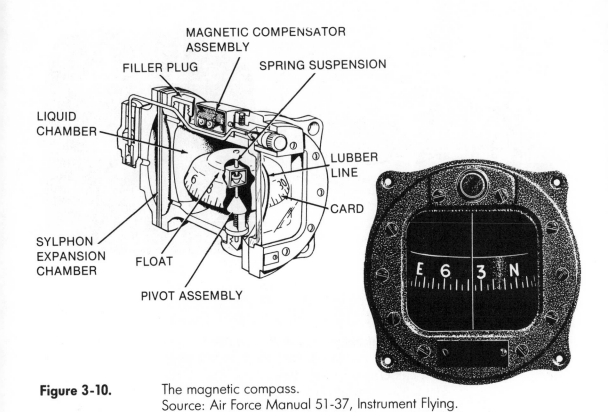

MAGNETIC COMPENSATOR
ASSEMBLY

FILLER PLUG   SPRING SUSPENSION

LIQUID
CHAMBER

LUBBER
LINE

CARD

SYLPHON
EXPANSION
CHAMBER   FLOAT

PIVOT ASSEMBLY

Figure 3-10.   The magnetic compass.
Source: Air Force Manual 51-37, Instrument Flying.

instrument indicator stable during periods of turbulent flight which would ordinarily upset the magnetic compass. Some directional gyros are purely mechanical devices, set by reference to the magnetic compass and then reset periodically. Others are tied in directly with a magnetic compass, usually located in a remote part of the aircraft, and give you a magnetic read-out, but one which is stabilized by a gyroscopic mechanism.

Turn and slip indicator—"the needle and airball." The turn and slip indicator was one of the very first flight instruments, and for years it was the only available reference for determining bank attitude (Figure 3-12a). More modern instruments have overtaken it for use in basic instrument flight (Figure 3-12b). It is now used primarily as a means of indicating the rate of coordination of a turn.

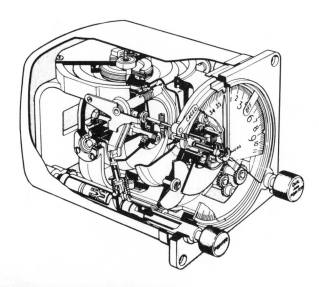

Figure 3-11.   Directional indicator.
Source: Air Force Manual 51-37, Instrument Flying.

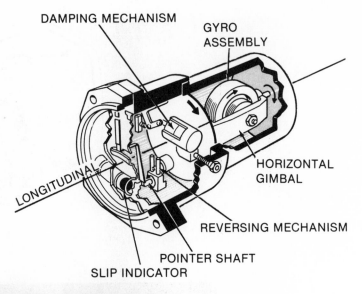

DAMPING MECHANISM

GYRO ASSEMBLY

HORIZONTAL GIMBAL

LONGITUDINAL

REVERSING MECHANISM

POINTER SHAFT

SLIP INDICATOR

Figure 3-12a.   Turn and slip indicator.
Source: Air Force Manual 51-37, Instrument Flying.

It is also an indispensable back-up should the more sophisticated instruments fail.

The turn needle indicates the rate of turn (the number of degrees per second an airplane turns), while the ball, which is located in a simple liquid-filled inclinometer, indicates whether the turn is being made in a smooth and coordinated manner. If it is, the

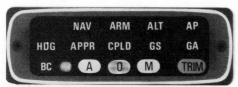

KA 285 Integral Mode Annunciator

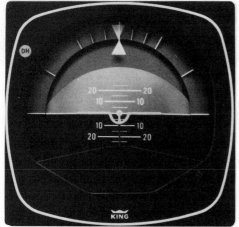

KG 258 Attitude Horizon Indicator

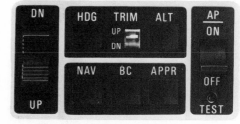

KC 292 Autopilot Controller

KI 525A Pictorial Navigation Indicator

Figure 3-12b. The KAP Autopilot. Equipment like this from King Radio Corporation makes life easier for a modern pilot. Shown is an integrated system of an autopilot, attitude horizon indicator, and pictorial navigation indicator. Reliable and lightweight, this equipment reflects an enormous amount of research.
Courtesy: King Radio Corporation

KNS 80 INTEGRATED NAVIGATION SYSTEM (VOR/DME/RNAV/ILS)

NAV & GS RECEIVER

DME

COMPUTER BOARD

Figure 3-12c. The secret of modern avionics lies in the miniaturized circuitry, which reduces both size and weight to the point that any light plane can be completely equipped without performance penalty. This is the King Silver Crown Integrated Navigation System.
Courtesy: King Radio Corporation

ball stays firmly in the center of the race, kept there by the smooth application of centrifugal force. If you *skid* (that is, fail to coordinate the rate of turn properly with sufficient angle of bank), the ball moves to the outside of the turn. If you *slip* (that is, use too great an angle of bank for the rate of turn), the ball slips to the inside of the turn.

In *either case,* "step on the ball" to correct the situation, that is, apply rudder pressure on the side the ball is lying. You'll be

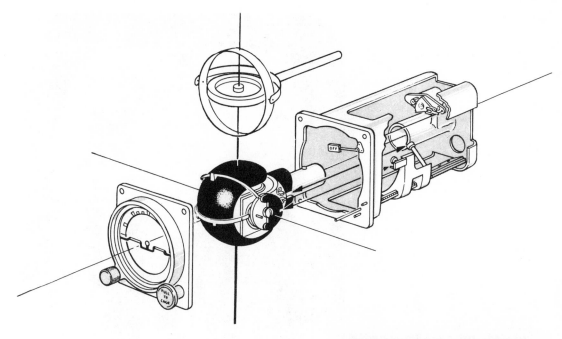

Figure 3-13a.   Attitude indicator.
Source: Air Force Manual 51-37, Instrument Flying.

Figure 3-13b.   A modern Bendix attitude indicator. While the instruments shown in 13-3a are a little dated, they serve to show the fundamentals of this piece of equipment. This modem instrument is designed and colored to be easier to interpret.
Courtesy: Bendix Avionics Division

amazed and gratified how just a little extra pressure on the rudder slides the ball right back to the center—and how much of an extreme comfort it is to the seat of your pants.

Attitude indicators. The principal unit for instrument flight in the trainers you'll be using is the attitude indicator, once known by a nicer name, the "artificial horizon." (See Figure 3-13.) By means of gyroscopes and a precise method of setting and calibration, the attitude indicator depicts the relationship of the aircraft to the real, actual horizon. When the aircraft is in a climb, with its nose lifted above the perceived real horizon, a similar indication is presented on the face of the instrument. The attitude indicator also reflects the angle of bank, and it is extremely useful as a cross-reference instrument even when you are flying "contact," that is, not on instruments.

Basic engine instruments The basic engine instruments include a tachometer, manifold pressure gauge, oil pressure indicator, oil temperature indicator, and cylinder head temperature indicator.

The measurement of power

Two instruments measure the power of an aircraft's engine/propeller combination.

They must be used together to obtain a proper reading and the best results from the engine. The *tachometer*, which measures the revolutions per minute of the engine, is familiar to most sports car drivers and serves an equally important but slightly different purpose. In an automobile, a tachometer can be used to determine "shift points," as well as to determine the upper safe operating limits. In an aircraft, tachometers are used to determine power settings for various modes of flight, and they are invariably used in conjunction with a manifold pressure gauge. The *manifold pressure gauge* literally shows the amount of power being packed into the engine, measuring it in terms of "inches of mercury," just as a barometer reflects barometric pressure in "inches of mercury."

Each aircraft has definite combinations of tachometer and manifold pressure settings for each mode of flight, from takeoff through climb, cruise, descent, and so on. In addition, a manual mixture control, which regulates the "richness" of the fuel-air mixture admitted to the engine by the carburetor, has a schedule of settings to correspond to the tachometer/manifold pressure gauge settings.

While this instrument may sound hopelessly complex on reading, it is not in practice, for there are relatively few settings to use and they generally make sense. For instance, you will use—naturally enough—a full, rich mixture setting for a full-power takeoff and a reduced, or leaner, mixture setting for cruising at reduced power.

Temperature and pressure readings

Oil pressure is a much more vital instrument in the operation of an aircraft than it is in a car. Obviously, an engine failure at altitude is a little more discomforting than an engine failure at Third and

Main. Also, however, aircraft engines are required to operate at a much higher level of power output than an automobile engine. Oil pressure and oil temperature are critical elements in engine operation, and they are presented on easy-to-read gauges, appropriately marked to let you know what is "in the green" or the safe range and what is "in the red," the dangerous range.

The cylinder head temperature corresponds to the engine coolant temperature gauge in a car and, like the oil gauges, is marked with a scale that clearly defines safe and unsafe operating ranges.

Instructors, however, are not content to let you look at the markings on the gauges to determine the prescribed operating ranges of each instrument. They expect you to know and understand exactly what each instrument is telling you about engine operation.

"All other" instruments

Among the "all other" instruments you will find a host of instruments covering a large variety of functions. There may be a vacuum pressure gauge, if you still have some vacuum-powered instruments. And there will be ammeters, a carburetor air temperature gauge, navigation instruments, and so on.

Unlike some instrumentation in automobiles—tachometers on a car with an automatic transmission, for example—every instrument or switch in an airplane has a legitimate, if not always vital, purpose. The cockpit time you spend in the early days of your training pays off when you learn what each of the items does, and why.

How to Make a Perfect Flight

Because flying *isn't* done out of a book, it comes incrementally, in small doses that the instructor knows you can handle. You start off with the four fundamental elements that make up all flying maneuvers—straight and level flight, turns, climbs, and glides. Then you gradually combine these in carefully designed exercises until you are fully qualified. This chapter explains the mechanical motions you will make in flying (although you won't be making them mechanically, but with fluid grace, of course) and gives you all sorts of little hints that you'll hear time and time again in your instruction. Don't expect to remember them all at once, but they will be more meaningful if you read them now and experience them later.

If you are serious about learning to fly, you'll want to do a number of things besides reading this and some other books listed in the back. First, you should arrange with your instructor to get a couple of hours of "cockpit time" in the aircraft in which you'll be receiving instruction. Many instructors will suggest doing so to you, while others may not feel it is necessary. If you do it, you will find it pays big dividends, for it enhances your instructor's comments to you. You'll be able to concentrate on the sense of what he's saying rather than trying to figure out which instrument he's referring to.

Second, take the handbook of the airplane—the owner's manual—and study it carefully, trying to understand how the various systems work and firmly fixing in your mind the prescribed airspeeds, temperatures, and so on. With the handbook before you, spend the cockpit time physically touching each switch and moving each control—but be sure to learn from your instructor which switches you may actually manipulate and which you may only touch. You wouldn't want to turn the mag switch on, for example, or move the retractable gear switch to the up position, even with power off. It's just not good practice to do so.

Continue this practice during your flight training any time you have had an interruption due to scheduling problems or bad weather. You can't imagine how reassuring it is to look instinctively at the right gauge or touch the right switch when your instructor calls on you to do so. If you have to hem and haw and search around, you'll find that the airplane begins "to get ahead of you" and your troubles will compound.

The perfect flight, step by step

Let's go through a perfect flight, relating the physical things you do in moving controls or switches for their desired effects. We'll also include, **in bold face,** certain basic truths, aphorisms, and even superstitions that you should carefully study and remember.

The perfect flight begins the night before, with a sound meal (no gargantuan adventures at Tippy's Taco House), no drinking, and a good night's sleep. The myth of the hard-drinking expert pilot is just that, a myth; pilots who drink before flying are not experts, but chumps.

Get to the airport early, for nothing dooms the enjoyment of a flight more than haste. Check the weather at length, fill out the forms, and carefully inspect the airplane. **Be sure you have a good breakfast,** because the judgment called for in flying can be impaired by what the doctors call hypoglycemia, or a shortage of blood sugar brought about by fasting.

The exterior inspection and every other phase of the flight **must be conducted with a checklist.** This rule is fundamental, because anyone, even a 40,000-hour airline captain, can forget a single item, and this could be crucial. It is another professional touch; good pilots use checklists even though they could dispense with them and do the inspection from memory. An engine start checklist is included at the end of the chapter; it shows you just how easy it is to do things correctly (Figure 4-1).

With the engine started, checklist completed, and radio call made, you are ready to taxi out to the runway. Release the parking brakes by pressing the brake pedals slightly. If the airplane doesn't begin to roll forward, you may have to add just a little power to get it started. Once it starts to roll, immediately retard your power to idle and **check your brakes.** The time to find out that you have brake problems is when you have almost zero speed, in the parking slot.

Brakes checked, let the plane roll forward a little before you begin your turn. **Never try to turn the nose wheel with the airplane**

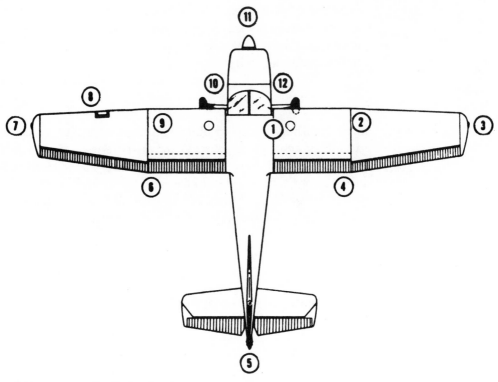

Figure 4-1.   Preflight check.
Source: Flight Instructor, Airplane, Written Test Guide AC 51-72
(Federal Aviation Administration).

1. a. Check quantity of fuel (2 gages).
   b. Make sure battery and ignition switches are "OFF."
   c. If fuel gage showed "FULL," remove fuel tank cap and check fuel level visually.

2. Check right wing for skin damages.

3. Check navigational light for damage.

4. a. Remove control surface lock, if installed.
   b. Check aileron and flap hinges.

5. a. Remove control surface lock, if installed.
   b. Inspect tail surfaces for dents, cracks, etc. Check surface hinges for cracks and hinge bolts for security.
   c. Inspect tailwheel spring, steering arms, steering chains, and tire inflation.
   d. Check tail light for damage.

6. a. Remove control surface locks if installed.
   b. Check aileron and flap hinges.

7. Check navigation light for damage.

8. Check landing light windows for security and cleanliness.

9. a. Remove pitot tube cover, if installed.
   b. Inspect pitot tube opening for stoppage.
   c. Check left wing for skin damage.

10. a. Inspect main landing gear wheel and brake fairing. Check tire for cuts, bruises, and proper inflation.
    b. Inspect airspeed static source hole on left side of fuselage for stoppage.
    c. Check oil level. Do not operate with less than nine quarts. Fill to twelve quarts for extended flight. For floatplane, refer to "OIL LEVEL," paragraph in Section I.
    d. Inspect cowl access doors for security.
    e. On first flight of day, drain a two-ounce quantity of fuel from the fuel strainer to check for the presence of water and sediment.
    f. Check cowl flaps for security.

11. a. Check propeller and spinner for nicks and security.
    b. Examine propeller for oil leakage.
    c. In cold weather, pull propeller through two revolutions.

12. a. Inspect cowl access door for security.
    b. Inspect airspeed static source hole on right side of fuselage for stoppage.
    c. Inspect main landing gear wheel and brake fairing. Check tires for cuts, bruises, and proper inflation.
    d. Check windshield and cabin windows for cleanliness.

at rest; it puts severe side-loads on the tire and the landing gear. In turning the airplane, anticipate the degree and the radius of the turn required by the size and shape of your airplane. If the parking area is crowded, get someone to "walk your wings." Any bystander will be glad to walk along your wing tip to make sure you get past a narrow spot; in fact, anyone standing there will probably have already volunteered to do so. **There is never any excuse for a taxi accident, day or night.**

As you taxi, keep the use of your brakes to a minimum by carrying the minimum power necessary to move at a slow, steady speed. You'll need varying amounts of power, depending on whether you are taxiing upwind or downwind or, in some airports, uphill or downhill. Also keep your eyes out of the cockpit. Watch both sides of the taxiway, and keep a look forward for other traffic that may be approaching from the opposite direction or from a collateral taxiway.

If something requires your attention—an abnormal engine gauge reading or the map falling off the seat—taxi to the side, set the parking brakes, and remedy the situation at rest. **Don't try to taxi and do other things—especially checklists—at the same time.**

Besides affecting your speed, the wind makes a difference in the control of the aircraft, for the broad side areas of an airplane give it a tendency to "weathercock" into the wind. Your instructor will show you how to hold the controls to your best advantage for the particular airplane.

You'll have taxied down into the run-up area for the runway that you are going to use for takeoff. Park at an angle that permits you a good view of other traffic and that also faces as much into the wind as possible. Carefully go through your warm-up and pre-takeoff checklists, as swiftly as you can do without sacrificing precision. Take whatever time you need, but courtesy demands that you be familiar enough with your aircraft and its procedures that you don't unduly delay the aircraft next in line behind you.

When your checks are completed, the tower (if the field you are using has one) checks you into position for takeoff. If there is no tower, you have to judge yourself when you should move onto the runway. In either case **you are responsible for checking the area to be sure you are not going to interfere with landing traffic,** which has the right of way.

Taxi to the very edge of the runway, so you have its full length to use. Any instructor will tell you, time and time again, **the two most useless things in the world are altitude above you and runway behind you.** Take advantage of the full length of the runway, even though it may be 10,000 feet long and you know that your takeoff run won't exceed 1,200 feet. It is mighty comforting to know that you can make your takeoff and still, in the event of an engine problem, land on the runway remaining ahead of you.

Takeoff   Line up with the centerline of the runway, make one last check of your instruments, and start the throttle forward, applying power in a smooth, steady push. The airplane immediately comes alive, a living creature. Keeping the airplane going straight requires you to push in a little on the right rudder, for the torque forces generated by the power plant tend to "yaw" the airplane to the left.

As speed builds, the wings begin to generate lift, and you can feel the airplane grow lighter on its wheels. Apply just a little back-pressure to establish the proper pitch attitude, and within seconds the airplane lifts itself off the ground, accelerating as it does so.

Your tasks immediately after takeoff are simple. Keep the wings straight and level, and establish an attitude that keeps the airspeed at your desired climb speed, say 70 knots indicated airspeed. Don't be in a hurry to turn out into the pattern, to make a power reduction, to make radio calls, or to do anything else. Concentrate on keeping your flight path straight along a line extended from the runway center line, and if the wind is drafting you off, make a correction by turning slightly into the direction of the wind.

Each field has prescribed approach and departure patterns, and most call for your first turn to be 90° to the left, starting the turn at an altitude of 400 feet above the ground. Just as in taxiing and for the remainder of the flight until you climb out of the airplane on the parking ramp, keep your eyes out of the cockpit, looking for other traffic. **There is no excuse for a mid-air collision.** A 45° turn in the opposite direction takes you out of the airport traffic pattern, and you can continue your climb to altitude. At 4,000 feet you level off and begin an element of your training so fundamental that it is often underemphasized—straight and level flight.

Level out and fly right

When you level out from a climb, you have to make a number of adjustments. First, you lower the nose by pushing forward slightly on the control column, and you begin to trim away the aerodynamic pressures you feel by using the trim tab. Because your cruise speed is always higher than your climb speed, you leave the throttle advanced for a while, accelerating to the 110-knot speed that you intend to fly. At about 109 knots, you reduce your power setting by pulling your throttle back. In the time it takes to do this, your speed has built to the desired 110 knots.

The reduction in power calls for another trim change, and retrimming the aircraft is necessary until you are flying straight and level at 4,000 feet, 110 knots, **hands off.** Always check your flight condition by releasing the controls and noting what the airplane does. It is very easy to sit and unconsciously apply control pressures instead of trim; doing so is not only fatiguing, it is a spring-loaded problem, for as soon as you release the manual pressures, the airplane starts doing what it has been trying to do all along. The solution is to trim as required so that the plane flies as you want it to, hands off the controls.

After you've established yourself in well-trimmed, straight and level flight, you can experiment with the controls to experience their individual and combined effects in flight, both through the seat of your pants and visually.

Just flying straight and level can be a satisfying flying experience. A perfect flight is not only doing everything correctly, and understanding just what is happening. It also consists of looking down from above on a world of multi-colored patches, tiny beetle-like cars, beautiful ponds, scudding clouds, and terraced towns. It is knowing that you are fulfilling not only your own dream, but the dream of the centuries. It is pure pleasure.

Let's depart a little from our well set-up situation by pushing in hard on the left rudder—just the left rudder, no aileron, no back pressure. The aircraft's nose skids around, you feel uncomfortable in the seat of your pants, and the telltale ball in your turn indicator instrument skids wildly to the right. The nose may dip slightly, and the airplane generally protests the treatment. After you release the rudder pressure, the plane cycles through some oscillations and gradually drifts back to straight and level flight, on whatever heading that happens to result.

Now let's use the aileron alone. Crank the wheel to the right, and what happens? The right wing goes down, but the nose tends to maintain its line of flight and turns, only grudgingly, into a skid that sends the ball to the right again. Release the aileron pressure, the wing comes up, and, after a few mild gyrations, you're back in straight and level flight.

Next just combine a little aileron and a little rudder, bringing both controls in together, and watching the nose of the airplane as it turns smoothly around the horizon. The ball stays centered in the turn and slip indicator. If you sense the nose coming down, either by reference outside to the horizon or by a loss of altitude on the altimeter, you gently correct by applying a little back pressure, increasing the pitch attitude.

Note that once the turn is established with the amount of bank you desire, you relax pressure on both the aileron and rudder, and simply fly the airplane around the turn with controls neutralized. When you wish to roll out, apply the controls in the opposite direction, anticipating that as you begin to roll level, you have to relax the back pressure you applied originally.

The secret of smooth flying is anticipation. Understand what maneuver you are going to do, and plan your control inputs so that they come together in an unhurried manner, in time for the controls to take the desired effect. If you have banked the airplane into a medium turn of, say, 20°, then begin your recovery from the turn about 10° prior to your desired compass heading.

Now take a look at the effects of the elevator on straight and level flight. If you are all trimmed up and pull back on the control column, you begin to climb. The nose of the aircraft rises above the accustomed spot on the horizon, and you begin to gain altitude and lose airspeed. If you take your hands off the control column, the airplane noses down and, after a few up and down oscillations, returns to straight and level flight at the altitude you departed. The reverse is true if you apply forward elevator pressure—you dive, gain speed, and then, when pressure is removed, oscillate back up to your attitude. This is the result of the aircraft's dynamic stability.

In the most basic terms, you are managing the energy of the weight and speed of the aircraft. Once you stabilize it at a certain speed and altitude, it tends to return to the same condition after any temporary displacement of the controls.

Something else happens if you affect one of the energy factors. If, from straight and level flight, you reduce the power by retarding the throttle, the aircraft noses over into a descent, maintaining about the same speed (although a very clean aircraft might accelerate) and losing altitude at a steady rate. Conversely, if you add power, the aircraft noses up into a climb and maintains this climb until it reaches a new equilibrium point for the power.

These exercises reemphasize a number of things about the airplane and yourself, the most important of which is that **you are in control.** The airplane, within its capabilities, does exactly what you want it to do.

Gain a little altitude—or the right way to get high

After your exercise reminds you how sweet it is to fly straight and level, you may want to climb to a higher altitude to be sure you clear the low deck of scattered clouds building up nearby. You already know that you can gain altitude simply by pulling back on the control column but that, without added power, you'd soon lose speed and eventually stop climbing.

Starting a climb from straight and level flight begins, then, with an increase of power simultaneous with the raising of the nose to the desired climb attitude. You notice that the horizon, which once stretched along just over the top of the engine cowling, is now even or just below the top of the cowling. Practice comparing a desired climb situation—that is, correct power, airspeed, and rate of climb—with the attitude of the aircraft. You are soon able to place the nose of the aircraft exactly where you want it with respect to the horizon, and your desired rate of climb is established automatically.

Because you changed the attitude of the aircraft and increased power, there are some changes in trim. You note that the ball in the turn and bank has moved slightly to the right, indicating that you should add some right rudder. If the climb is going to be a long one, you can trim out the back pressure, so that the airplane climbs hands off, just as it flew straight and level hands off. As you climb, atmospheric pressure decreases, and so does the power produced by your engine. To compensate, you have to occasionally add a little more throttle.

When you approach your desired altitude—say 5,000 feet—the first step is to start to lower the nose, anticipating the lag time of the instruments so that you level out precisely at 5,000. Leave your power up for a while, so that your airspeed builds back up to your desired cruise speed. Note the attitude of the aircraft relative to the real horizon (and for comparison, to the attitude indicator). When the airspeed is at the desired point, reduce your power.

As soon as you level out, you feel changes in control pressures, and you use the trim tab to relieve these. There are additional trim changes when you reduce power.

Take a dive— the right way

The movies of the 1930s were filled with scenes of heroic test pilots hurling their aircraft straight down and pulling out in a (you'll pardon the expression) gut-wrenching 9-G wing-breaker. Chances are you'll never have to get your nose much lower than 30° below the horizon, and most of the time you'll make descents at an even more gradual angle. Still, there's a right way and a wrong way.

If you wish to lose a thousand feet of altitude, you do not, oddly enough, simply reverse the technique used in the climb. There are some important differences, relating to the way the engine operates and to the fact that gravity never stops working. Before you start a glide, on most airplanes you have to pull the carburetor heat knob out to the "On" position. Some advanced airplanes don't have carburetor heat, but let's assume that yours does. Next, close the throttle as much as you think you need to achieve the desired rate of descent. If you want to go down fast, bring it back all the way; if you want to ease down a couple of hundred feet per minute, just retard it a few inches. Then, instead of applying forward pressure to go down, you find yourself applying back pressure, to keep the nose at the desired point below the horizon and to give you the speed and rate of descent that you want. A normal rate means the nose of the aircraft is just a little farther below the horizon than it is in normal straight and level flight.

If you glide for long distances, **clear the engine with short bursts of power;** this prevents it from "loading up" and perhaps not running properly when you level out.

As always, trim the airplane so that it glides hands off. Leveling off from a dive involves the same kind of anticipation as did leveling off from a climb. Close your carburetor heat knob, advance the throttle, and begin your level-off 50 feet or so above the desired altitude. With a little practice, you'll wind up exactly on altitude and airspeed.

Put them all together, they spell everything

You've just gone through a series of maneuvers in which you did very well in straight and level flight, turns, climbs, and glides. You have the fundamental skill to do any maneuver—it's simply a matter of putting the elements together in a smooth, coordinated fashion.

Note of caution   As your proficiency grows and as you begin to combine the various maneuvers well in gliding turns, spirals, climbing turns, chandelles, lazy eights, and so on, you'll be tempted to get a little ahead of the program and try some aerobatics. Just a simple loop, perhaps, or a barrel roll—it looks so easy, and a hot pilot like yourself should have no trouble.

Don't do it. Aerobatics are great for building confidence and proficiency, but you need to have instruction from a certified flight instructor, or you'll get yourself into trouble. Acrobatics, like any other maneuver, are an extension of fundamentals, but they place you and the aircraft in situations that can disorient you if you aren't sure what you are doing. Once disoriented, you may inadvertently place stresses on the airplane that it was not designed to take, causing it to break up in flight.

I really encourage you to take an aerobatic course, if you are interested, but *don't* fool around on your own. Once you've taken the course, you'll see why.

A little showing off   The only acceptable way to show off in an airplane is to fly it with cool professionalism. Hot-rocks who think they are showing off by flying low or chancing a roll over the airport, or who make their patterns to the field too low and too tight, are showing off only their ignorance. You are still on your perfect flight—show off to yourself by putting all the elements together in a precise flight back to the field and a beautiful landing.

But showing off has some other, less dramatic aspects. You sometimes show off only to yourself when you skip a procedure to save a little time. Other temptations to show off occur when, despite bad weather, the airplane's unsafe condition, or your ill health, you choose to fly because of some compelling reason or another to take the trip. A typical case might be a salesman, new to flying as an aid to his business, out on a trip with his boss, pleased to be able to show him how efficient it is to cover his territory with an airplane. Late in the afternoon the weather reports begin to sour, with reports of thunderstorms in the area of the airport that the boss wants to reach that night. Big moral question: Can you tell the boss you are afraid to fly, even when it may mean that he won't be able to close a deal? Yes, hell yes, anytime and every time.

Confidence Is the Key

Never undertake anything in an airplane that you don't feel fully confident with. The same philosophy applies to maintenance: If you don't like the way the engine sounds, even if there is no other indication of a fault, don't take the airplane up.

Sometimes minor things are bothersome, but they really don't seem important enough to "abort" a flight. Usually, something is slightly disturbing. **Beware of a sequence of two or three minor items.** Problems tend to accumulate. Most accidents are not the result of a single cause but rather a culmination of a series of untoward events, any of which individually isnot serious.

Remember, you are in command of the airplane, and very likely no mission you are called on to fly is worth an accident. Don't let false pride trip you up. Okay, back to the flight.

Down we dive

Dive gently, of course, for you want to descend to the traffic pattern altitude without flying through anyone (Figure 4-2). All airports have prescribed approach and departure procedures. All traffic is expected to use the pattern created for takeoffs and landings. The pattern is rectangular, consisting of (1) the *downwind leg,* which is used to establish landing traffic in a sequence, and (2) a *base leg,* 90° to the downwind, which allows you to lose altitude and to position yourself for the turn to the final approach. A specific height—say 800 feet above the ground—is prescribed for the downwind leg, while a *minimum* height is prescribed for the turn to final. The positions at which the turns to base and to final are made depend both on traffic and the wind. In a no-traffic, no-wind situation, you can make a 90° turn to base and a 90° turn to final. If a great deal of wind is blowing straight down the runway, your turn to base may be much more than 90° and your turn to final may be slightly steeper.

Entry to and departure from the traffic pattern is always done in the published manner—for the best of reasons, collision avoid-

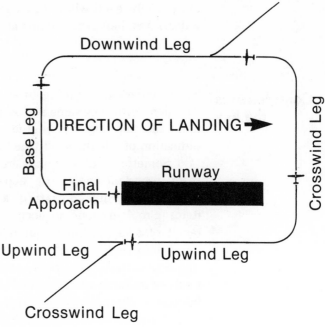

Downwind Leg

Base Leg

DIRECTION OF LANDING ➤

Crosswind Leg

Final
Approach

Runway

Upwind Leg   Upwind Leg

Crosswind Leg

Figure 4-2.   Standard traffic pattern.
Source: Flight Instructor, Airplane, Written Test Guide AC 61-72
(Federal Aviation Administration).

ance. Entry is almost always made a mile or two from the field, depending on the amount of traffic, and it can be made at a 45° angle to the downwind leg or on the upwind entry leg (Figure 4-2). Before entering the pattern, particularly when descending to the pattern altitude, you should check very carefully below and ahead of you, making clearing turns to be absolutely sure that you won't run into anyone.

Bring the airplane to a low cruise speed, say 110 knots, and make preliminary radio checks to advise the tower of your intention to land and to learn what other aircraft are in the pattern. Position your plane behind the next, at a distance that permits the plane in front to land and to **clear the runway** before yours is ready to land.

You should try to turn from the 45° entry leg to the downwind leg at a point where your wing tip traces a line just along the edge of the runway. This turn is a little difficult at first, but after awhile you pick up visual clues from the ground that give you landmarks for turning. **Don't grow to depend on these, however.** Each time you enter the pattern, even if you are right over your landmark, note the relative distance from the airport as it appears to you in the cockpit. This perception assists you in establishing your position at other airports where you don't have landmarks all picked out.

Get set up early on the downwind by having your airspeed nailed down to the figure called for in your manual—today, let's say it's 100 knots—and go through your pre-landing checklist, all the while maintaining a vigilant lookout for all aircraft, particularly the one in front of you. You not only don't want to run into it, but the pilot will give you clues as to how soon you can land. If he or she carries the pattern out too far, you're obliged to position yourself behind him; if he is able to make a close-in pattern, you'll be able to follow. If he suddenly "goes around," that is, doesn't land, but instead climbs back up into the traffic pattern, you have to investigate and perhaps follow suit. **Never be ashamed to go around.**

As you pass the end of the runway on the downwind leg, you begin your preparations for the next part of the pattern, the base leg. Normally, if everyone is positioned well, you may retard your throttle just as you begin a turn to the base leg. Because you are flying downwind, plan to turn just a little more than 90°, so you can compensate for the wind drifting you. After you cut the throttle, apply a little back pressure and ease the aircraft to its best glide speed for the base leg—90 knots in this case.

Keep the wind in mind at all times. The wind is a constantly changing variable in the landing game, and it plays a vital role in establishing a proper pattern. In a very strong wind, you may have to angle the base leg in towards the field. Your goal is to fly the aircraft through the air in such a manner that you compensate for the wind effect and describe a ground track that is perpendicular to the runway.

Depending on the airplane, you may or may not make your first flap setting on the downwind leg. Adjust your flap setting on the base to help position the aircraft in both height and distance for the turn to final. If you are far out and low, do not put anymore flaps on; if you are close in and high, put down half or full flaps.

The turn from base to final is controlled by your computer-like brain integrating a number of facts—your altitude, airspeed, distance from the field, the direction and speed of the wind. Complicated as it sounds, the problem is really a rather simple and most satisfying one to solve, for the correct turn from base to final puts you directly on an imaginary line drawn out from the center of the runway.

The quality of the landing is determined by the quality of the pattern. You will not make consistently good landings if you do not fly the pattern at the correct altitudes and airspeeds and at the correct distance from the aircraft you are following. Most students make the mistake of worrying about and working hardest over the last ten or fifteen seconds of a landing attempt, trying to touch down smoothly after they've been all over the sky on the downwind and the base. You soon find that a correctly flown pattern results almost automatically in a good landing.

Almost—some skill and finesse are still involved in touching down properly. As you come down the final, your flaps set, your throttle at idle, the back pressure trimmed off the controls so that the air speed stays steady at 80 knots, you can concentrate on what is often the pay-off for the entire flight, a smooth touchdown. The smooth touchdown begins with a gentle round-out or flare of the aircraft, the beginning of the smooth arc that changes the linear descent on the final into a mating with the runway. As you begin your round-out, your airspeed decreases and the nose of the aircraft rises slightly. Maintain back pressure on the control column, letting the aircraft settle, and keep it flying straight down the runway with the appropriate use of the ailerons and rudder. The aircraft settles to the runway, main wheels first, as you continue to maintain back pressure. Just as the airspeed drops to the stalling speed, your wheels touch down. Keep the back pressure on till the plane slows, then gently lower the nose wheel to the ground.

Easy, wasn't it?

One difficult thing for students to learn on landings is where to look. The natural tendency is to look right over the nose of the plane, perhaps twenty or thirty feet in front. But your eyes simply cannot accommodate to the speed of the aircraft in this situation, and you lose all your depth perception—and, in effect, your ability to see how high off the runway the airplane actually is. The solution is to look down the runway to the far end, and to keep looking there all through the landing flare and touchdown. Your visual mechanism picks up cues from the attitude of the aircraft and its relation to the field that enables you to determine your relative height above the ground to within a few inches.

Once the airplane is slowed to a safe speed, turn it off the runway as soon as possible as a courtesy to aircraft landing behind you.

Now that you see how easy it is, we ought to try to get you a private license. Come on.

Notes to chapter four   Checklists vary from two or three short pages for a light plane to voluminous books for a transport or bomber. The following is a short annotated checklist for the engine start of a Piper Cherokee.

Starting engine

1. *Set parking brake on.* Conceivably you could hold the brakes with pressure on the pedals, but your attention might get distracted and the airplane could move forward.

2. *Set carburetor heat control in the full "Cold" (off) position.* Almost certainly it will already be in that position, but you always check.

3. *Select desired tank with fuel selector valve.* The Cherokee has two 25-gallon tanks; select the tank that has more gas in it. You will have already visually checked the level of the gas in the tank against the reading on the fuel quantity gauge.

4. *Starting a cold engine:*

   a. *Open throttle approximately one-quarter inch.* This positions the carburetor control so that enough fuel is metered to start the engine, but not so much as to cause it to "race."

   b. *Turn master switch "On."* The master switch is, just as the name implies, a switch that controls electricity to all parts of the aircraft.

   c. *Turn electric fuel pump "On."* The electric auxiliary fuel pump pushes gasoline up from the tanks to the carburetor.

   d. *Move mixture control to "Full Rich."* This control permits fuel to enter the carburetor.

   e. *Engage starter by rotating magneto switch clockwise and pressing in.* This establishes the supply of current to energize the starter and furnish electricity for the spark plugs.

f. *When engine fires, advance throttle to desired setting.*

That's it. This little exercise with the checklist is not to teach you how to start engines, but instead to show you how easy the use of a checklist makes the mechanics of flying. Without checklists, the whole procedure of start, takeoff, and landing seems hopelessly complicated. With it, it is merely a matter of learning a series of sequenced operations.

The engine starts, you check the oil pressure to see that it is coming up, and then you retard the throttle to the desired rpm— 1,000 or so. If you have accurately positioned the throttle for the start, only a little advance is required to establish the 1,000-rpm setting desired for warm-up. Be cautious that the engine doesn't race to too high a setting—1,500 rpm, for example—for this causes undue wear on the engine.

If the engine does not fire within three to five seconds, then disengage the starter, prime the engine with two or three strokes of the priming pump, and repeat the starting procedure. Unlike an automobile engine, where you can engage the starter for almost as long as the battery will stand it, an airplane engine places an extremely heavy load on the starter. If you keep it continuously engaged, you will burn it out. A well-tuned airplane starts relatively easily; if it doesn't, you should have it examined by a mechanic to find out why.

How-to books   You can't really learn to fly from them, but they can really help you learn to fly. Following are some of the better "how-to" books, listed only by title and author because they are available from so many different sources.

Anyone Can Fly, Jules Bergman. Well-written, well-illustrated.

Private Pilot's Dictionary and Handbook, Kirk Polking. Good reference.

The New Private Pilot, Zweng. Good basic information.

Understanding Flying, Richard L. Taylor. Simple approach to some complex subjects.

Student Pilot's Manual, William K. Kershner. All of Kershner's books are outstanding.

Stick & Rudder, Wolfgang Langewiesche. Dated but still worthwhile.

Flying Safely, Richard Collins. Basic tips on surviving in flying.

Getting Your Ticket

It is relatively easy to fool yourself when glancing in the mirror. Tuck in the old tum, chin up, chest up and out, eyes squinted up a bit—and you can kid yourself into thinking that you are ten years younger. And you can fool yourself at the dinner table too, taking an extra slice of pie on the strength of your tucked-in tummy.

But you can't fool yourself in an airplane. If ever there was a place where the truth is clinical, it is when you sit alone in the cockpit, the engine shut down, the myriad noises of an airplane cooling off crackling in your ears. In those few private moments you know exactly how well or how poorly you flew that day.

What do you have to do to reach the point where you can enjoy this intimate self-knowledge? First of all, get a certificate as a private pilot. The FARs—Federal Aviation Regulations—are precise on the minimum requirements: You have to be at least 17 years old, be able to read and speak English, be medically qualified, and pass certain written and flight test requirements. In addition, you need at least 40 hours total of dual instruction and solo flight time, broken down in certain ways well covered in FAR part 61.

But much more important, you must have found a flight instructor who can safely impart the necessary knowledge to fly. The instructor-student relationship is incredibly important, and the time spent in seeking out the right instructor more than pays for itself.

What should you look for? First of all, seek a flying school that has obvious stability and permanence. You don't want to start out with one instructor, and find that his or her firm has folded. Check the back of the chapter for some of the better known schools, and also look in the advertisements in magazines like *Flying*. Check with the FAA and the yellow pages too. You don't have to go to the biggest school in the area, but carefully check out the one you choose. Call the Better Business Bureau, and see if the firms you are interested in have a good reputation. Ask the school for the names and phone numbers of satisfied customers.

The instructor you choose should be friendly and obviously

able to communicate. Don't get lined up with a taciturn type, for you are going to need someone who is able to point out your mistakes in a way you'll understand. Similarly, watch out for super-glib super-salestypes, for they may tell you more than you want to hear at any one time.

Most instructors are glad to spend time talking with you before you ever sign up; if they aren't, don't even bother with them. Ask pointed questions—where did they go to flying school, how many hours do they have, how many students have they trained, where have they worked, what kind of aircraft are they checked out in, what rating do they have, and so on. If you do this in a polite, interested manner, they won't be offended, and they will probably be pleased at the chance to brag a little bit. Often the oldest, highest-time pilot isn't the best instructor, nor is even the best pilot necessarily the best instructor. The single most important quality, besides the ability to fly with the competence necessary to receive an instructor's certificate, is the instructor's personal interest in the student's success.

The student-instructor relationship is inherently complex. On one hand, the student is hiring the services of both the instructor and the plane; on the other, the instructor is placing his life and valuable aircraft in totally unknown and as yet unskilled hands. This interdependence alone is sufficient for stress. Added to this are the ordinary differences in personality, outlook, value systems, and the like that occur between any two people.

Fortunately, most of the problems implicit in the situation are overcome by the instructor's professional attitude and the student's inveterate desire to please. Nothing is more important to the instructor than seeing you safely on your way to a flying career; when other instructors give you a check ride or when you go for a flight check with the FAA, you represent your instructor, who wants you to do well. The greatest reward a flight instructor receives is to know that he has taught you to fly better than he can!

Long before this, however, hours of dual isntruction time pass, while you learn and make mistakes and while the instructor corrects you. He demonstrates a maneuver, you goof it up, and he demonstrates it again. During this process, the true, long-term relationship develops. You discover that you've picked a winner among instructors when he can analyze the pattern of your mistakes and tell you not *what* you are doing wrong, but *why* you are doing it and how to correct it.

In most instances a friendship grows between a student and instructor, one that the student tends to remember far longer, for you have few instructors, while the instructor has hundreds of students. But during the period of flight training, the student pilot develops a regard for the instructor that is unlike that felt for any other person in his or her life. The instructor is someone who can teach what the student desperately desires to know: how to fly. In teaching, he can dispense sweet rewards of praise (at least once in a while, anyway) and give pointed words of criticism; and *both* are eagerly awaited. An odd business.

The student-instructor relationship has changed drastically for the better over the last fifteen years, going from the sadomasochistic style that prevailed almost from Kitty Hawk to a sensible, psychologically well-founded system. In the very early days of flight, hapless novice pilots were dragooned into being instructors. With sometimes only forty or fifty hours total flying time, they were expected to pass on their newly acquired knowledge to even less knowledgeable students. An instructor with fifty to one hundred hours flying time could not have been any more comfortable instructing in 1916 than in 1926 or 1946 or 1976; he simply didn't have enough experience to be confident of his control of the aircraft.

To hide this deficiency, it became common practice for instructors to bully, berate, and haze students, criticizing them continuously, banging their knees black and blue with the stick, abusing them over the oneway "Gosport" communication tube, and in general behaving in an immature, beastly fashion. If the student was able to keep his wits about him and make some progress, he was turned loose to solo only after a final vile session, during which the instructor would confide that he preferred the student to die alone and was therefore getting out of the airplane before his next landing. This cruel, often sadistic style persisted for years. It was a rare military instructor pilot who, sensitive to his students' needs, tried to find out what the problems were and to counsel him effectively.

The brawling macho mystique was excused for a variety of reasons. It was done "to see how the student did under pressure" or to "force the student to divide his attention." Baloney! There is enough stress in a new student's cockpit for anyone, and a continuous barrage of insults from the instructor is the last thing required.

One of the results of this Neanderthal approach was a colossal "wash-out" rate at flying schools. The rate varied with the urgency of ever-changing pilot requirements or the war situation, going from a high of 100 percent wash-outs in times of victory to as low as 40 percent when pilots were badly needed. This tragic waste embittered a lot of young men who would have become fine pilots, and it threw away millions of taxpayers' dollars.

My own first flight instructor, a middle-sized grinning young man who could have passed for James Garner, has given me the cold shudders for years. Not too long ago I would involuntarily curse at the mention of his name—Paul Dupree. (That's not it—no sense getting into a libel suit.)

On our very first day at the flight line, the day we had been awaiting so eagerly for months, we found out that one of us was going to wash out—and fast. It seems that the instructor didn't believe he could do a good job of instructing five students at a time—or perhaps he was too lazy to do so—and he was going to wash one out immediately so he could do a good job on the remaining four. I drew the short straw, and nothing I did pleased the man. He failed me on two out of my first three rides. One more failure would have meant an automatic check-ride and probably a passport to flying oblivion. By a freak of fate, another student insisted on transferring from his instructor, and we were swapped. Three rides later, he was gone, and I never had another failing ride.

The psychological trauma of military flight training was carried over to civilian pilot training. But civilian training was harsh to a lesser degree, because, instead of having a captive audience of hot, young, eager Kaydets all trying to win their wings—and stay out of the infantry—civilian instructors were businessmen who had to beat the bushes for paying customers. Yet the abrasive techniques lingered on for longer than they should have, and they still do to some extent. You *don't* have to put up with it.

Mercifully, most of this went out the window after about 1960, when it finally penetrated the GI psychology that browbeating a student was counterproductive and that intelligent, human-relations-oriented instruction was needed. As a result, both civilian and military flight training offer an essentially pleasant, thrilling experience. If at any time in your training you don't find it to be so, you should immediately look around for another flight instructor.

The moral of this, of course, is that an instructor is out there who is right for you and who will make learning to fly pleasant. Don't settle for less.

The intricate pattern of the student-instructor relationship begins at their first meeting and builds steadily to the initial solo flight. In the course of eight to twelve hours, you get to know each other very well, practicing landings, emergencies, stalls, and so on. The time comes when the instructor must decide whether it is safe for you to take the airplane up by yourself.

Here the reasons for faith, trust, and total honesty on the part of both student and instructor are made manifest. You, the student, risk your life on the instructor's assessment of your ability and judgment. The instructor, besides a natural concern for you as a human being, places an objective value on the airplane and upon his reputation as an instructor. The student-instructor relationship becomes more than synergistic; it is symbiotic, and the first solo is a major psychic reward for both parties. The instructor teaches, observes, evaluates, and deems you ready to solo.

The evaluation is a cumulative one, established on the last six or seven flights. He notes how hard you work, how well you do, whether you know what you should know from the pilot's handbook, how often you repeat the same mistakes, and so on. Not a single phase in your short career isn't measured from first taxi to last shutdown; it's all been marked in his memory.

A good instructor keeps this ceaseless evaluation from you, for it can drive you crazy, wondering what he is thinking about. And the process works both ways. For your part, you have noted when the instructor refrains from comment when you made a dumb mistake or when he turns your grief at a bounced landing into a smile. You'll check his judgment, too. Does he practice what he preaches? Does he curse when another student gets in your way in the landing pattern? Or does he look pained if you are running late for a take-off but still have to go back and attend to a call of Nature? He shows off a little too, making an occasional landing to "show you how it's done" or executing a steep 360° turn that bumps you solidly in your own wake turbulence.

On your own   When time has passed, your skills improve and you begin to have a little confidence in your ability. Your thoughts turn to the possibility of going solo. It comes about in an off-hand manner, about half way through a dual flight. After some airwork and a few landings, the instructor tells you to pull off the taxiway and suggests that you take the airplane around yourself. He has a few upbeat comments, tells you what to watch out for, and asks you to make three landings, no more, and then to bring the aircraft back to the parking area. Then he gets out and walks away—to watch surreptitiously from the edge of the hangar.

Suddenly the airplane feels funny, for you are in it alone for the first time. The narrow cockpit, much too chummy on a hot day with an instructor aboard, is now quite spacious. Visibility is better, and, mercifully, no one watches you wipe the sweat off your hands.

After a good checklist-type run-up, you taxi out and find that takeoff is easier solo than dual. Sensing that the instructor's 170 pounds is missing, the trainer leaps off the ground a little earlier.

And that leap is the moment you've been waiting for. The wheels leave the ground, and you are flying the airplane solo. It's up to you. No one's there. You do the same things you've done fifty times before, but you can't help noticing that no one's there but you. A glance at the wings, thrusting with force upon the invisible air, and you realize that—hot damn!—you're a pilot!

Unfortunately, there is only one "first solo." If you never fly again, you've soloed. And that means you are a pilot.

There is the little matter of landing, of course, but that'll be a piece of cake too. Even though you want to do well and "grease" it in like an airline pilot, it doesn't really matter as long as you get down safely and in one piece.

And you do, and you do it twice more, and the day seems perfect. It takes iron self-control not to smirk idiotically as you taxi back to the line and see your instructor sauntering toward you, giving the high sign, so why bother? Smirk, grin, simper—you've soloed, and you've earned every iota of pleasure you can wring from the process. The instructor is grinning too, for not only does he know exactly how you feel, but he also feels pretty good himself, for he's launched another pilot into the blue—and gotten him back!

In some ways the first solo is very much akin to the loss of virginity: It is an irrevocable act, a dividing line, a boundary, a new life. Its passage is marked by a number of rites, ranging from being thrown bodily into the swimming pool to having a necktie or a shirttail cut. You'll find that the glow of the first solo barely subsides when it's back for more dual instruction, with a decided difference. You are no longer a complete tyro, a novice, for you've passed a big hurdle, and you'll note a subtle change in your instructor's manner. It's sort of like going off probation, all the way to temporary status.

As the flying hours build, there will be a succession of events similar to the first solo. Some are not quite so heady, but two—the first solo cross-country and the actual attainment of a private certificate—are just about equivalent.

First solo cross-country

The first of these, along about the twentieth to twenty-fifth hour, is the first solo cross-country. This is a big step, for it involves landing at an airport more than 50 nautical miles from the point of departure and landings at two airports that you haven't seen before. It includes the full gamut of flying from flight planning, through checking the weather, to navigating by pilotage—using time and distance checks against visible checkpoints.

You'll probably be pretty comfortable in the airplane by the time the first "XC" rolls around, and you will have had dual cross-country work with your instructor. Still, it's a lonesome but good feeling when you walk alone to the airplane, armed with a checklist, a map, a computer, and a quiet prayer for direct headwinds and tailwinds.

In the ordinary airwork around the airport, the winds are only a minor consideration. They force you to concentrate when you are practicing turns around a point, and, of course, you have to determine their direction carefully before landing. A bad cross wind, uncorrected, can ruin an otherwise perfect landing. But on cross-country work you realize clearly that your three-dimensional truck driving is taking place in a moving ocean of air and that pointing your aircraft's nose at a distant target does not necessarily get you to it.

In a no-wind condition, or when the wind is directly from the nose (headwind) or tail (tailwind) of your aircraft, the plane follows a precise track through the sky from point to point. The track is identical, given good piloting, to the one you plotted on the map. But when there is a wind from the side, the airplane drifts with it; if no corrective action is taken, the airplane moves in an angular fashion, its nose pointed one way and its actual movement another.

But you can correct for drift, simply by turning the nose of the airplane into the wind and "crabbing." Now the airplane follows the same straight flight path over the ground that it did in a no-wind condition, but it does so with the nose of the airplane cocked to one side.

Normally, a solo cross-country starts off even more pleasantly than a first solo. After all, you have a little time in the airplane now, you can land it, and the first twenty minutes of a cross-country flight are in a familiar territory surrounding the home airport. You've carefully laid out a course on the map, just as you did on the dual work; beside the penciled lines are your notations about distinctive features on the surface, called *checkpoints*, where you can match the symbols on the map with the actual ground terrain.

As inspiring as the first solo flight was, it came about so rapidly and was over so quickly that it scarcely had time to register. On the solo cross-country you have time to contemplate your mastery of the air. The engine runs smoothly, the compass doesn't swing, you hold your altitude to the foot. Things are going well, and perhaps for the first time since you started flying you relax, just a little.

It's ten minutes to the next checkpoint, a perfectly defined intersection of a railroad and a highway, and the wind seems to be about as predicted; blowing steadily from the left, at about 20 mph and at an angle of perhaps 60° to your flight path. You cock the nose to the left to correct for the wind drift and press on.

After another five minutes you begin to look ahead for the checkpoint, a beauty, for not only does it feature the perfect X of the railroad-highway crossing, but there is a horseshoe-shaped lake just to the left of the intersection.

But after a few more minutes, there is one small problem: The lake isn't there, and the highway and the railroad seem to run parallel instead of crossing.

Panic! Immediate panic! Where's the lake? What's the course? What's the wind? What are you doing there?

Then the amused, reassuring voice of your instructor comes flooding back into your memory: "Don't panic. Keep flying the same heading. See what landmarks you can identify from the ground to the map. Verify that you are flying the right course. *Don't panic, don't panic, don't panic.* Check the wind, check your airspeed, check your watch."

He's right, of course, even in absentia. A small factory is down below helpfully violating environmental protection laws by spewing out a thick white smoke that is blowing in just the opposite direction to the one you'd planned on. A large light goes off! You've corrected in the wrong direction for the wind. It's been blowing from the right, and you've turned to the left and must be well left of course.

A right turn of 30°, and in just a few minutes, there is something shimmering on the horizon. It's the horseshoe lake, and there, just as promised, is the beautiful intersection. It's the checkpoint, all right, but now you have to scramble to refigure your ground speed (way low, because the checkpoint is still ahead of you, even after your correction) and to make the course correction in the right direction for the next leg of the trip.

The beauty of a little trauma like this is that it teaches you the difference between mechanical flight planning and mechanical flight, and genuine flight planning and the actual flight. On paper you can move swiftly from point to point with the flick of a plotter; in real life you have to take into consideration all three dimensions of flight, plus a fourth: chance. In addition, there are the vagaries of the wind and weather, as well as the very real possibility of mistakes by the pilot.

There are more rewards en route, for one of the real pleasures of a first or any cross-country is the fascination of landing at an unfamiliar airport. For one thing, you have to try harder to fly a good traffic pattern, because no familiar landmarks tell you where to enter on your downwind leg. For another, you don't have an established set of visual clues to tell you where you are in relationship to the ground when you begin your round-out.

After landing, it is all pleasure, however, for you have the opportunity to eyeball all the airplanes on the ramp, checking out any unusual ones—that Howard DGA-15 over there, for example—with care. You can then casually amble into the flight operations shack to have your log signed to verify that you have, in fact, come this far.

Cross-countries are almost as much fun as shooting landings, and they bear the closest resemblance to the type of flying you may later do as a businessman or, with electronic assistance, as an airline pilot.

With a successful solo cross-country behind you, you are in the midst of the final drive toward the third and, in some ways, most important goal, attaining a private pilot's certificate. Just as the instructor's attitude changed somewhat after you soloed, so is it altered, matured even, in this latter stage. He is confident that you have the capability to achieve a pilot's certificate. He wants simply to be sure that he teaches you the right things, that you apply yourself in the correct manner, and that you pass all the pertinent written and flight tests.

The written test may well seem to be the biggest problem, for a formidable amount of material has to be learned. But if you have been diligent all along, studying as you went, you shouldn't have any problem. Various booklets, put out by the FAA (such as the Private Pilot Examination Guide) as well as by some private concerns, walk you through the format of the tests, asking typical questions.

The FAA also now publishes all the test questions, so that it is theoretically possible to review them all in advance. Practically, this is difficult. And, of course, the real point is not knowing the answer to a specific FAA test question, but knowing the material from which the FAA question is derived, and being able to apply that knowledge to flying.

Several commercial schools also give intensive weekend courses on the material to be covered in the tests. This sort of cramming is popular and helpful, if you have put in plenty of home study. And if you can afford it, you should consider it. It is not absolutely necessary, however, if you really study the material that is given you as a part of the course. More than anything else, it conditions you to the types of questions asked rather than providing a "crib" of information.

Your flight training is more demanding. Almost no time is wasted from takeoff to landing, for your instructor asks you to make takeoffs under different conditions (short field, soft field, half flaps, and so on), and you do emergency procedures on every flight. But even as closely as he watches and critiques your performance of flight maneuvers, he is assessing your judgment even more. He doesn't want to recommend a pilot who can do all the maneuvers perfectly but who hasn't the judgment to carefully pre-flight, to keep track of the weather, or to behave courteously in the traffic pattern.

Curiously, your flight check is a time of great psychic pressure on your instructor. He wants you to succeed for your own sake, but a certain amount of self-interest is involved, too, for he wants the FAA inspector (a member of the local flight standard District Office, or FSDO) to approve of him as an instructor. A bad student ride is not just a bad student ride on a check flight; it means an instructor may have not done his job properly, perhaps making the instructor an object of FAA concern.

The actual flight check can be a pleasant experience if you and your instructor have properly prepared yourselves with adequate training and adequate knowledge of the paperwork involved. Flight check pilots are simply businessmen, doing what they are paid for, and they have certain minimum standards for performance. You can make errors—everybody does on every flight—but you shouldn't make too many of them, nor should they be of the dangerous kind.

And if you should fail the flight check, don't be too embarrassed or discouraged. A lot of people have failed, and most have passed on subsequent re-examination. Sometimes a series of chance coincidences prevents an instructor from covering a certain point with a student adequately. Or perhaps a student performs certain maneuvers well by chance without really understanding how to do them. On the check ride, with its change of pilots, circumstances, and often even airports, the stress of the ride can cause the student to be unable to do something that he's done right before and thus fail the test as a result. Remember, you are only human.

The chances are that you'll pass and pass with gratifying ease, changing over from being a student, an aspirant, to a full-fledged, certificated pilot—who knows he has a lot to learn.

Now what about the cost—has it been worth it? The answer depends on lots of things. First of all, the cost varies from flying school to flying school, from instructor to instructor, and from student to student. But on the average the complete cost of ground school (usually incorporated in the flying school fee), flight instruction, physical, books, and the like runs around $1,800 to $2,000. That is not an inconsiderable sum of money, but let's put it into perspective: The lower figure of $1,800 is about the difference in prices between a medium-sized car, say a Cutlass, and a subcompact, like a Monza. It represents two weeks in Hawaii, fifteen days in London, or, if you are unlucky, one night in Vegas. It also represents several suits of clothes and an overcoat. It is an excellent stereo set and one of those instant replay television outfits.

But all these items are ephemeral; you forget the time in Hawaii, the car wears out, the stereo is replaced by quadra-sound. But the private pilot's certificate is yours forever, a treasure to keep, irrefutable proof of your accomplishments in the sky. And it can be a ticket to a lifelong hobby or to a host of new careers as a commercial pilot in either general aviation or with the airlines. It is a tangible return on your investment.

Before making a decision on either of these fields, let's take a look at where they've been, where they are, and where they are going, so that you can determine what your preference is.

For more information

The best place to get full information on Federal Aviation Administration requirements is from the FAA manuals themselves, which are available from the U.S. Government Printing Office, Superintendent of Documents, Washington, D.C. 20402.

The publications are well-done, and are furnished at what must be cost or less than cost, considering the generally inflated price of books today. Write for their catalog entitled "Aviation Information and Training Manuals," which lists all the current, pertinent publications.

Following is a partial listing, showing the manuals that you ought to have for openers:

Federal Aviation Regulation, Part 61,	($2.90)
Certification: Pilots and Flight	
Instructors	
Flight Test Guides:	
Private and Commercial Pilot, Free Balloon	($1.10)
Private and Commercial Pilot, Glider	($1.50)
Private Pilot, Airplane	($1.35)
Flight Training Handbook	($2.15)
Pilot's Handbook of Aeronautical Knowledge	($5.30)
Pilot's Weight and Balance Handbook	($2.30)
Student Pilot Guide	($1.50)
Weather for Aircrews	($2.80)
Written Test Guides:	
Private Pilot, Airplane	($2.30)
Instrument Rating, Airplane	($3.75)

There are a host of others, and of course, there are revisions to content— and to prices—periodically.

Where to go for training

The schools on the following list have excellent, well-equipped training programs. They have been chosen for their reputation, capabilities, programmed training, and geographical location. There are many other schools of comparable quality for you to investigate, as well as many smaller fixed-base operations that do a fine job of flight instruction. You will have to be the one to judge.

American Flyers, Incorporated
Ardmore Airpark, P. O. Box 3241
Ardmore, Oklahoma 73401
(405) 389-5471

Century Aviation
Dulles International Airport
P. O. Box 17323
Washington, D.C. 20041
(703) 471-1677

Embry-Riddle Aeronautical University
Daytona Beach, Florida 32014
(904) 252-5561

Florida Institute of Technology
School of Aeronautics
P. O. Drawer 1839
Melbourne, Florida 32901

Sierra Academy of Aeronautics
Oakland International Airport
Oakland, California 94614
(415) 568-6100

Parks College of St. Louis University
Cahokia, Illinois 62206

Spartan School of Aeronautics
International Airport
8820 East Pine Street
P. O. Box 51133
Tulsa, Oklahoma 74151

If you are not so much interested in a flying career as a career in flying, you should check out the following:

Northrop University
1162 W. Arbor Vitae Street
Inglewood, California 90306

Pittsburgh Institute of Aeronautics
P. O. Box 10897
Pittsburgh, Pennsylvania 15236

Probable costs for a private pilot certificate

A typical private pilot's certificate will cost *approximately* $2,000, if you attend one of the schools just listed.

These costs break down, *roughly*, into the following:

Classroom preparation	$ 400
Flight training:	
25 hours dual	$ 900
25 hours solo	$ 480
5 hours ground instruction	$ 50
Total	$1,830

The average student may require more flight training than the 50 hours listed to achieve a license; if so, costs will go up.

A set of sample questions

The following questions are taken from the *Private Pilot—Airplane Written Test Guide*, published by the Federal Aviation Administration. For each rating, similar lists of questions are published. The idea, of course, is not to memorize the questions which may not appear on any test in exactly the same form, but instead to become familiar with the content of the material from which the questions are drawn.

You'll note that beside each question there is an alphanumeric code. The code indicates the source for the answer to the question.

In question 049, for example, "C07" stands for Federal Aviation Regulation Part 91, General Operating Rules, Subpart A, "Liquor and Drugs."

The study guides also contain extensive bibliographies of recommended study materials.

048. Is it permissible for a pilot to allow a person who is obviously under the influence of intoxicating liquors or drugs to be carried aboard an aircraft? This is permitted

CO7 1- only if the person does not have access to the cockpit or pilot's compartment.

2- only if the person is a medical patient under proper care.

3- only after a waiver has been obtained from the FAA.

4- under no circumstances.

049. No person may act as a crewmember of a civil aircraft if that person has consumed any alcoholic beverages within the preceding

CO7 1- 8 hours.

2- 10 hours.

3- 16 hours.

4- 24 hours.

050. In addition to other preflight action for a VFR cross-country flight, regulations specifically require the pilot in command to

CO3 1- determine runway lengths at the airports of intended use.

2- check each fuel tank visually to ensure that it is always filled to capacity.

3- file a flight plan for the proposed flight.

4- perform a VOR equipment accuracy check prior to the proposed flight.

051. Preflight action as required by regulations for all flights away from the vicinity of an airport shall include a study of the weather, taking into consideration fuel requirements, and

CO3 1- an alternate course of action if the flight cannot be completed as planned.

2- the filing of a flight plan.

3- the designation of an alternate airport.

4- an operational check of your navigation radios.

052. In addition to other preflight action for a VFR cross-country flight, regulations specifically require the pilot in command to

CO3 1- file a flight plan for the proposed flight.

2- check each fuel tank visually to ensure that it is always filled to capacity.

3- determine runway lengths at the airports of intended use.

4- check the accuracy of the omninavigational equipment if the flight is to be made on airways.

053. In your preflight action for a cross-country flight, if you obtain only the Aviation Weather (Hourly Sequence) Reports and do not utilize available forecasts, you are

CO3 1- violating regulations by not also reviewing the weather forecasts.

2- exercising poor judgment but not violating regulations.

3- adhering to regulations since the pilot in command is not required to check forecasts.

4- adhering to regulations unless the flight is being conducted in interstate air commerce.

054. In addition to other preflight action, regulations specifically require that, for VFR flights not in the vicinity of an airport, the pilot in command shall determine

CO3 1- that aircraft and engine logbooks are aboard the aircraft.

2- alternatives avaialble if the planned flight cannot be completed.

3- visually that each fuel tank is always filled to capacity.

4- the accuracy of the omnireceiver if airways are to be flown.

055. When two aircraft are approaching each other head-on or nearly so, which aircraft should give way?

DO3 1- Regardless of the aircraft categories, a glider has the right-of-way over all engine-driven aircraft.

2- If the aircraft are of different categories, an airship would have the right-of-way over a helicopter.

3- Regardless of the aircraft categories, the pilot of each aircraft shall alter course to the right.

4- If the aircraft are of different categories, an airship would have the right-of-way over an airplane.

056. Assume two aircraft of different categories are converging at approximately the same altitude. Which of the following is a true statement?

DO3 1- Neither aircraft has the right-of-way and both aircraft should alter course to avert a collision.

2- An aircraft towing or refueling other aircraft has the right-of-way over all other engine-driven aircraft.

3- An airship has the right-of-way over a glider.

4- A jet airliner has the right-of-way over all other aircraft.

057. In order to determine when the battery of an Emergency Locator Transmitter (ELT) will need replacement, regulations require that the expiration date be

C35 1- listed on the Airworthiness Certificate.

2- marked on the aircraft instrument panel placard.

3- marked on the outside of the transmitter.

4- listed in the engine logbook.

058. When are Emergency Locator Transmitter (ELT) batteries required to be replaced or recharged?

C35 1- Every 6 months.

2- After 100 cumulative hours of use.

3- After 30 cumulative minutes of use.

4- After 1 cumulative hour of use.

059. Which statement is true concerning an Emergency Locator Transmitter (ELT) aboard an airplane?

C35 1- ELT battery replacement is required after each ten hours of cumulative use.

2- When activated, an ELT transmits on the frequencies 118.0 and 122.3 MHz.

3- An operable ELT is required on all training airplanes operated within 50 miles of the point of origin of the flight.

4- Tests of the equipment should be conducted during the first five minutes after every hour.

060. When activated, an Emergency Locator Transmitter (ELT) transmits simultaneously on which of the following frequencies?

C35 1- 118.0 and 118.8 MHz.

2- 121.5 and 243.0 MHz.

3- 123.0 and 119.0 MHz.

4- 122.3 and 122.8 MHz.

061. Unless each occupant is provided with supplemental oxygen, no person may operate a civil aircraft of U.S. registry above a cabin pressure altitude of

C22 1- 10,000 feet MSL.

2- 12,500 feet MSL.

3- 14,000 feet MSL.

4- 15,000 feet MSL.

062. When operating an aircraft at cabin pressure altitudes above 12,500 feet MSL up to and including 14,000 feet MSL, supplemental oxygen shall be used

C22 1- at no required time by a private pilot.

2- while at those altitudes for 15 minutes.

3- during the entire flight time at those altitudes.

4- while at those altitudes for more than 30 minutes.

General Aviation

At Kitty Hawk, in 1903, there was only "general aviation," and for years afterwards the only distinction might have been between "military aviation" and "general aviation." But as aviation specialties grew, so did the requirement for better definitions. In recent years, aviation has been divided roughly into "military" and "civil," with the "civil" further subdivided into "air transportation" and "general aviation." The latter category now includes all flying other than commercial passenger and freight flights.

However, a case has been recently made that the civil category should be redefined to specify "air transportation" and "recreational flying." The rationale is simple enough: The business pilot, bent on getting executives, special parts, insecticides, or whatever from point A to point B, is engaged in air transportation, while the recreational pilot—the student, the weekender, the antiquer, the glider pilot—simply doesn't need the same navigational equipment, communication facilities, airport aids, and, especially, regulations that the other group does.

Underlying all this is a growing antagonism among the vested interests of airlines, executive transports, and recreational pilots over the use of airports, airspace, and so on. The tragic crash in San Diego, in which a PSA 727 overran a Cessna, underlined the problem and heightened the growing demand for a solution to the dual use of the airspace.

General aviation is unbelievably healthy. Although statistics are terribly boring, more than 200,000 general aviation aircraft are projected for the 1980s, versus perhaps 2,000 to 2,500 airliners. General aviation factories are expected to produce 20,000 new aircraft annually. More than 40,000,000 hours will be flown per year, and there will be perhaps 780,000 to 800,000 pilots. This state of affairs is almost unbelievable, given how slowly general aviation started. It had the fastest conception and longest gestation in history.

The origins of general aviation

Immediately after World War I, the flying world was a mass of contradictions. Facile writers, fanning a tremendous interest in aviation, saw commercial airlines connecting every point in the U.S. and envisaged simplified "flivver" airplanes in every garage. The writers were abetted in this by manufacturers like Curtiss, Dayton-Wright, Orenco, and others, who had made a great deal of money during the war building—or trying to build—warplanes and who had set up substantial, expensive manufacturing bases. They *needed* to believe that there was a commercial requirement for their wares, and they naturally tried to sell the public and the government on this belief. Typically these companies offered a line of aircraft similar to the line of automobiles that manufacturers conjured up then and now. They offered trainers, sportplanes, "broughams," "limousines," and so on, in the hope that somehow the public would respond in the same golden way that it did to automobiles.

And the inevitable promoters invented an airplane or an airline or an aircraft manufacturing concern with the same ease that they sold underwater lots in Florida. It was actually easier, for they usually fastened onto some sincere, well-motivated designer who believed the promoters' claims and who wanted desperately to see his newest airplane produced. As a result of these combined genuine and fraudulent promotions, the public developed the notion that somehow the Golden Age of Aviation was just around the corner and that there was a real requirement for the airborne transportation of passengers and cargo, as well as many special business applications.

Working against these commendable, if highly inflated, expectations were a number of hard, hard facts, some totally unrelated to aviation.

First, the United States had an extremely efficient allweather rail system whose crack trains could actually achieve "ground speeds" in excess of the top speeds of many of the airplanes of the time. In these days, when we compare jet travel with the sometimes pathetic efforts of Amtrak, we forget how efficient the rails of the 1920s were, with good service, comfort, safety, and a sense of serious, enduring responsibility. The railroads were formidable competitors, and they effectively strangled air travel at birth. It's instructive to note that in Europe, on the London to Paris run, for example, the aircraft of the time were able to compete much more effectively because the distance was relatively short and you thus avoided the train-boat-train connections. In the U.S., a comparable distance, say from New York to Washington, was a quick train ride from city-center to city-center, with a sure schedule, lots of departures, and a pleasant, heated club car en route. The difference became even more pronounced on long trips, especially in mountainous areas.

Backing up the rail system was a highway system, which, while primitive compared to today's sterile network of four lanes, clover leafs, CB radios, and Howard Johnsons, still offered tough competition to air travel. The trucking system, though still not fully matured, supplemented the rail network.

More important than either competitor was the fact that available aircraft were slow, short-ranged, unreliable, and restricted not only from instrument flight but often from flying at night. You could convert a de Havilland DH-4 observation plane from World War I into a passenger plane of sorts by roofing over the back cockpit with a leaky celluloid cover. But you could not convert the aging Liberty engine into a reliable power plant, or transform the pilot into a skilled instrument flyer, or materialize from thin air the necessary ground network of landing fields, lights, beacons, radios, and so on. The effect of these deficiencies was as great on general aviation as it was on commercial air travel.

Moreover, the public, with its great good sense, must have been aware that there was no regulation of any of the proposed services: Pilots were not licensed, planes were neither licensed nor inspected, routes were not sanctioned, and fields not built to any safety standard. Pilots with $500 could buy 50 hours of flight instruction and an airplane, and then go into any business they had the nerve to try.

But the damning and ultimately decisive factor was that no mass market existed for commercial aviation, either air transportation or general, because it was not yet profitable in time or money for either the shipper or the airline passenger to fly.

Nostalgia tends to make us forget that businesspersons were just as profit-oriented and competitive then as now—perhaps even more so. If a profit could have been made from the use of aircraft in any manner, they would have used them despite inconvenience, hazard, and other drawbacks. If you stop to compare the inherent difficulties of building a rail system in the nineteenth century—the vast distances involved, the enormous capital required, the hazards of climate, Indians, and the relatively primitive tools—with the difficulties of building an airline in the early twentieth century, you see at once that aviation was ignored not because of the problems involved but because of the lack of profit potential.

As a result, the only aviation that could endure was what some would like to call "recreational aviation"—nonprofit aviation. This situation, Eden-like as it may appear today, was intensely frustrating to the people who wished to make a living from aviation. The nonmilitary aviation activity that did exist did so as a result of investment money generated by the general prosperity of the times, which enabled company after company to appear, issue stock, sell one or two aircraft, and then disappear into bankruptcy. There was a very limited market for luxury aircraft, just as there was for Rolls Royce cars, no matter what the economic state. It was a custom market in which the wealth a man gained in his main occupation— real estate, oil, law, the stock market—could be applied to the conspicuous pursuit of a very expensive hobby. Only in very rare instances—some oil companies, the Huff-Daland Dusters (about which we"ll say more later), and a few others—did airplanes actually pay for themselves.

For the most part they were expensive luxuries, testimonies to the healthy egos of those who bought them. If you have a chance, go back to old library copies of *Sportsman Pilot* magazine and read about the Long Island Country Club of the Air, with its blue-blooded membership. Read the advertisements, which urge the extremely wealthy to buy the airborne equivalent of a yacht and limousine. Curiously, the situation is not too different today, for the substantial constituents of corporate reasoning in the purchase of executive aircraft are factors of prestige, ego, and "perks."

But certain events were to give general aviation a series of boosts. Unfortunately, unlike modern rocket boosters that lift a vehicle smoothly and safely into orbit, general aviation's boosts tended to be erratic and short-lived. While each helped it to reach its present glowing state, there were a number of interruptions.

The "Lucky Lindy" period The firsts of these boosts, one that looked as though it would take it cleanly (if I can abuse the metaphor) from the launch pad of World War I and all the way to the orbit of economic self-sufficiency, was the Lindbergh boom. Despite the mild case of "balloonamania" resulting from the Double Eagle II's first flight across the ocean and the 1977 celebration of the fiftieth anniversary of Lindbergh's epochal flight, we did not recapture even one percent of the hysterical ferment that gripped the country after May 21, 1927. We literally went aviation-mad, and there were a number of good psychological factors for this fever. It had been a long time since World War I heroes had returned, and the country was in the grip of a period that would later be graced by the title, "The Roaring Twenties." There were gangsters, speakeasies, prohibition, a mild recession, and then a vigorous, intoxicating boom. There was the Harding scandal, Sacco-Vanzetti, and the twin specters of Red Russia and run-away inflation in Europe. Into this climate of discontent stepped the bright young knight errant, the Lone Eagle, Lucky Lindy—Charles A. Lindbergh.

Coupled to this apparent answer to a national prayer was an abundance of capital, even though much of it was stock market "funny money." Investors were literally crying for investment opportunity, and Lindbergh seemed to have created one in aviation with a single flight.

Important technical factors also provided the nascent aviation boom with a basis in science. The most important of these was the development of the reliable air-cooled radial engine in the form of the Wright "Whirlwind." This engine was the product of the combined genius of many men, beginning with Charles Lawrance, who designed the *Lawrance J.*, a nine-cylinder radial engine that promised to free the Army and Navy from the handicaps and headaches of water-cooled engines. The most influential names in military and civil engine development—Commander Jerome Hunsaker, Admiral W. A. Moffett, Frederick Rentschler, George Meade, Andy Willgoos, Sam Heron, E. T. Jones, and others—combined to create an engine that would not only ultimately carry Lindbergh and the *Spirit of St. Louis* from New York to Paris but that would also provide the basis for an entire new crop of much more efficient airplanes. The *Whirlwind* engine in its several models (the *Spirit* used a J-5) was a remarkable advance over all engines then available to the public. Capable of 220 horsepower, relatively light, with none of the weight or other complications of its water-cooled rivals, the *Whirlwind* was exactly what the Liberty and Hispano-Suiza developments of the time were not—reliable and durable enough for commercial use.

In a similar manner and at the same time, the supply of World War I airframes had been exhausted, and a new group of aircraft, incorporating the structural and design refinements learned in the previous ten years, began to appear. Benefitting much from military experience, these aircraft still consisted basically on wooden wings and steel tube fuselages covered with fabric, but they were more streamlined and had the benefit of vastly improved airfoils, including the famous Clark "Y." They reflected the fact that the current design teams could much predict weight, drag, and lift factors more accurately than before and that they could utilize the advantages offered by the *Whirlwind* engine. Even the basic shape of the aircraft was beginning to change, although the biplane remained the preferred approach for most. The monoplane, primarily because of the influence of the Bellanca designs and the *Spirit of St. Louis,* was beginning to assert itself as the shape of the future.

And, less than coincidentally, the 1926 *Air Commerce Act* had provided a means by which funds from several federal department sources could be directed into such uncolorful but essential needs as beacons, weather services, preparation of airfields, and so on.

Thus the essential conditions for an aviation upturn already existed when Lindbergh landed at Le Bourget, and the American public was more than ready for a boom in general aviation. Lindbergh was the essential catalyst.

Two typical cases

Unfortunately, the boom was sustained primarily by the continual influx of speculative capital from the investment community; it did not sustain itself, as did the rail system, by profits generated from the safe, efficient transport of people and cargo. This point has been overlooked in history and in literature, and one can understand why. The contemporary literature points only to the entries into successes in the field. When a new aviation company was formed, a substantial part of its budget was dedicated to informing the world of its existence. There was always an elaborate public relations coverage of the new facilities, first flights, sales, deliveries, and so on. But when the company faded, as so many did, it was over a relatively long time. If any announcement was made of the firm's demise, it was usually a short paragraph buried somewhere in the back pages.

Let's look at a typical example of a firm that most people have never heard of, one that is entirely typical of the time. The EMSCO Corporation was founded in 1929, and the name of the firm derived from its principal backer, E. M. Smith. Smith was an industrialist with holdings in oil, machinery, asbestos, and many related fields. Like thousands of less well-financed individuals, he was convinced that aviation's time had come.

Smith was immensely far-sighted, and his choice of a plant site showed this perfectly. He bought seventy-three acres in Downey, California, and built a million-dollar aircraft factory before he had a single order for an airplane. (The plant itself still exists, having been first a part of Vultee, then North American, and finally Rockwell.) He hired the services of a famous pilot and designer, Charles Rocheville, as well as several other top people, and undertook the construction of a complete line of aircraft ranging from a handsome two-seat trainer to a four-engine transport.

EMSCO heralded its arrival on the aviation scene with a series of brilliant full-page advertisements in *Western Flyer*, *Aero Digest*, *Aviation*, and other leading business-oriented flying magazines. It looked like an invincible combination of talent, finances, and promotion.

The firm built sixteen aircraft and then folded, disappearing without a trace into the economic slump of the time. The failure was due in part to Smith's financial and tax problems, but the primary cause was that, despite the Lindbergh boom, there was no solid commercial market for aviation services. No matter how good, or how pretty the EMSCO aircraft were, no one bought them. (See Figure 6-1.) This harsh "no-need" situation completely countervened the public's enthusiasm for aviation, yet enthusiasm could not overcome the economic facts of life.

Of the rare exceptions to this typical lack of success, the most impressive example is that of Huff-Daland Dusters, Incorporated, the cropdusting firm whose instant commercial success led ultimately to the formation of today's Delta Air Lines. The story reflects in microcosm all the points I've been trying to make about general aviation: (1) General aviation could not develop successfully until it could generate a profit; (2) certain technological thresholds had to be reached before a profit could be generated; and (3) these technological thresholds could derive only as a spinoff from military aviation development.

Figure 6-1.   The EMSCO firm built 16 airplanes, all of them as beautiful as this Model B-2 built for Colonel Pablo Sidar. Unfortunately, no major market for the line developed, and it disappeared into history.
Source: Author's collection.

The firm was founded by Thomas Henri Huff and Elliot Daland in 1920, and it immediately began to build a series of the most godawful-looking airplanes the world has ever seen. There were no civil sales, and, in attempting to interest the struggling Army Air Service in their products, the company received an essential crash course in aircraft design. Huff-Daland submitted one abortive effort after another to the experts at McCook Field (The Dayton, Ohio, predecessor of both the modern Wright-Patterson and Edwards Air Force bases). And each time they did, the engineers there pointed out the many things wrong with it. Huff-Daland went back, redesigned the airplane, and resubmitted it for tests. Eventually, through a long iteration of failed tests and intelligent responses to the new information, Huff-Daland came up with an airplane that was in construction and appearance almost identical to the German Fokker D.VII of World War I.

From that point, even though aircraft of basically similar style and construction were being made in dozens of small factories all

Figure 6-2.   The plane that started what eventually became Delta Airlines . . . the Huff Daland Duster. It was successful because it could earn a profit. Courtesy: Delta Airlines

across the country, Huff-Daland found a commercial use for the plane, where it could earn a profit as a *tool* and not as a showpiece. The U.S. Army had been experimenting with aerial crop dusting for years, using Curtiss JN-4s and de Havilland DH-4s as duster planes. Huff-Daland, through their association with McCook Field, became intimately familiar with the task and designed an airplane specifically to spray crops with insecticide. They also formed Huff-Daland Dusters, Incorporated, to do the job.

They built eighteen duster planes and inaugurated an instantly successful business. In the first year, over 60,000 acres of Southern farm land, cotton, and peaches were dusted, at a cost of $7 per acre. It was a profitable operation from the start, and it soon expanded not only in the South but, in the off season, in South America. Huff-Daland Dusters, which under the guidance of C. E. Woolman eventually became Delta Air Lines, is the most dramatic example of the use of general aviation aircraft during the 1920s.

EMCSO and Huff-Daland illustrate perfectly the plight of general aviation through the Roaring Twenties and the early thirties. Flying was too expensive for the ordinary person and too inefficient for the businessperson. Only in very specialized cases was it a profitable investment possibility, a barrier that prevailed for years.

The model Ts of the air

Considering the built-in handicaps of general aviation, the full impact of the general worldwide depression of 1929 was bound to have catastrophic results. The first law of business, then as now, is that in times of recession the first things to go are the frills. And aircrafts were invariably regarded as frills. The plants and airfields that sprang up like mushrooms after a rain, just as quickly withered and died. Brave names that advertised boldly—Golden Eagle, Command-Aire, New Standard, Kreutzer, Mercury, Simplex, Doyle, Ireland, Davis, Star, and so on—were gone, and their dreams with them.

The residual development of general aviation in the depression years was driven into two main avenues. First, a few manufacturers managed to survive, turning out very expensive aircraft for an extremely limited market. After all, movie stars, like Wallace Beery and Robert Taylor, still flew. Record attempts were still made, and, at the very top, there was still some limited business use. The general market for aircraft of reasonable performance had dried, for planes were too expensive, and no profits were to be made.

Almost as if on a signal, manufacturers, in desperation, grasped at a second idea, the very low-cost light plane. If enough extremely inexpensive light planes with a low operation cost could be put into use, they might create a pool of pilots who might continue to fly when the depression ended and who would constitute a market for the larger, higher-profit, high-performance aircraft. Mixed into a jumbled mental association of the advertising man, the manufacturer, and the public was, of course, the Model T. The big question was, "Who would build the flying flivver?" Over the years a number of firms attempted to market light, low-powered aircraft in the U.S. without much success, even though these airplanes had become almost a national fad in England.

The most important U.S. example, of course, was the Aeronca C-2, designed by Jean Roché of Mc Cook Field, and destined to be the recognized ancestor of all American light planes. The Aeronca

C-2 was Roché's successful attempt to achieve a simple, inexpensive light plane that still met recognized aircraft engineering requirements. The spartan, stark little C-2 was built without amenities, its only instrument a tachometer. And instead of brakes the pilot reached out with a gloved hand and squeezed a wheel to slow it down after landing.

The Aeronca sold relatively well in 1929 and 1930, becoming the leading light plane. It was also one of the reasons that the giant Curtiss Wright Corporation jumped into the scene with its pusher Curtiss Junior, a curious aircraft to look at and not always pleasant to fly. Curtiss built 270 of them in a single year and then shut down production upon finding a dangerous spin characteristic under certain conditions. "Selling relatively well," however, requires some definition. America had a population of 120 million at the time, and despite the depression was still producing some 2 million cars a year. Light plane output was less than 500 per year, or only 0.00025 of auto production. Clearly general aviation had not yet reached the national consciousness where it mattered most—in the pocketbook.

However, two men were instrumental in changing the frustrated status of aircraft manufacturers. The first is C. G. Taylor, a young self-taught engineer who created the famous Taylor Cub as a direct rival to the Aeronca. C. G. Taylor is one of the many genius engineers who never really had the proper financial advisors and whose designs often made more money for others than for himself. The second, of course, is the famous William Piper, who went with Taylor through a series of financial reverses before buying him out in 1935.

The first Taylor Cub, the E-2. was similar in size to the Aeronca, but it was prettier and a better performer. Despite its advantages, very few were purchased—22 in 1932, 16 in 1933 and 70 in 1934. The problem was that Taylor was not a marketing man, and Piper had not yet applied his full talents to the company.

After the reorganization, which saw Taylor leave to found another firm, Piper evolved a simple marketing philosophy that made the Cub the dominant airplane in the marketplace. He determined to build one airplane, build it well, and sell it with conviction. He created a slogan for the Cub that he used to convince airport operators to buy it, and the slogan was simply this: "The Cub Will Make You Money." There, in a nutshell, was the whole secret behind making general aviation, or any enterprise, a success. You had to show people how to make money. And the Cub did make money, for it was inexpensive, rugged, simple to maintain, and attractive to look at in its bright yellow fabric. Being called "Cub" didn't hurt either, for it was just the right name for a trainer.

Piper continued to drum his sales methods into dealers around the country, and sales of the Cub began to climb in a manner totally new to the aviation scene. 210 Cubs were sold in 1935, more than twice that in 1936 and 687 in 1937. It seemed that at last, someone had found the formula for general aviation success. Its success seems all the more dramatic when you compare the costs of flying then and now. Nowadays we often think that the biggest drawback to learning to fly is its relatively high cost, with dual instruction running as much as $28 per hour. Back in 1932, flying lessons were often as high as $25 per hour, and even operators using the Cub were hard-pressed to keep costs down to $10 an hour. These prices prevailed at a time when porterhouse steak went for 25 cents a pound, new Chevrolets for $495, and a doctor, if he was lucky, made $3,000 a year. Despite the relatively high cost of flying, Piper achieved success.

The runaway success of the Cub naturally inspired competition. C. G. Taylor had not rested after being bought out by Piper, and he was engaged in the manufacture of the handsome Taylorcraft, essentially a Cub with side-by-side seating. Aeronca was still on the scene, changing from its bathtub-shaped Model C to the pugnacious-looking Model K and finally entering into an annual styling competition with Taylorcraft and Piper. This competition it almost always lost, much as Plymouth always trailed Ford and Chevrolet no matter how it innovated. Neither Aeronca nor Taylorcraft had Piper's marketing savvy, and consequently neither expanded sales at the same rate.

The Plymouth-Ford-Chevrolet analogy applies in other contexts as well, for most of the national advertising of the three leading light planes was couched in automotive terms, and this affiliation rubbed off on the styling touches. The manufacturers began making cockpits more automobile-like, adding over-sized plastic dashboards, chrome strips on the engine "grill," and so on. The purpose, of course, was to create the illusion that flying was basically no more complicated than driving and that everyone should have a plane.

Flying Cadillacs

The rest of general aviation continued in just about the same mode that it had pursued for years. Some excellent aircraft were built to serve the needs of wealthy sportsmen and the truly advanced thinkers in business. These include the Fairchild 24, Stinson Gull-wing, Cessna Air Master, Waco cabin planes, and, of course, the empress, the staggerwing Beech D-17S.

These remarkably handsome, efficient aircraft possessed a purity of line that makes them collector's items today. Their performance, in terms of what is today known as "block speeds," is so close to modern single-engine planes as to make you wonder about the exact extent of progress. The Beech B-17R staggerwing of 1935, for example, carried four persons at a maximum speed of 202 mph, cruised at 195, and had a range of 760 miles at cruise speed. The modern Bonanza (Model V35B) has a little higher top speed, cruises at 194 mph, and has a range of 716 mph—while carrying four passengers. The admittedly great differences in manufacturing and operation costs are not substantial enough to win the argument totally for the modern plane.

Another much more modern aircraft had also made its debut, and, although its worth was immediately recognized, years passed before it achieved a position of dominance in the business fleet, primarily because corporations were not ready to understand just how fine a performer it was. The revolutionary twin-engine Beech D-18, the first "twin Beech," entered production in 1937 and remained there through 1969, the longest production run of any aircraft until the Bonanza broke the record. The Bonanza began production in 1947.

The dubious benefits of war

All these advancements were soon overshadowed by the prospect of war. General aviation came to a virtual standstill with Pearl Harbor, but the manufacture of general aviation types soared as the military required them for trainers, liaison planes, and so on. Much more important in the long run than the increase in the manufacture of aircraft was the wholesale production of pilots. U.S. pilot training—and in fact worldwide pilot training—increased by orders of magnitude. It ultimately reached a point where too many were produced and where whole flying school classes were abruptly ordered not into the blue but into the infantry.

Almost inevitably aircraft manufacturing executives concluded that each of the returning pilots would demand to have a private plane of his own—a post-war boom. These hard-bitten executives, who had suffered years of disappointment scratching to make a living in aviation, fell into exactly the same trap that their forebears did one war previously. It is amusing now to read the almost lyrical predictions of 1944 and 1945, which showed an airplane in every garage and a helicopter in every backyard. Such projections were highlighted with artists' renditions of a smiling, handsome young man in a Fedora hat taking his light plane to work, with wife and two kids smiling a goodbye.

The assumption, once again, was that mass production of aircraft would reduce price to the point where the average man could elect to have an airplane just as he chose to have a family car. The war plants engaged in a tremendous conversion process, and in the first year after the war built 35,000 airplanes for the private market. Production dropped to 16,000 in 1947, to 3,500 in 1948, and all the way to 2,300 in 1951. The boom, once again, had collapsed, and general aviation was back in the doldrums.

The consequences of this repetition of history were incalculable. Nothing makes an industry more bitter, conservative, and less inclined to invest than a cataclysmic boom-and-bust cycle. General aviation found itself in a situation almost identical to the immediate pre-war period.

The delayed boom

But slowly, almost imperceptibly, certain economic factors outside the scope of general aviation were coming into play, factors that had a cumulative, positive, long-range effect and that made general aviation an attractive field today.

First of all, after a few fitful starts in the immediate post-war years, the United States was entering into an unprecedented period of almost uninterrupted prosperity. Despite occasional "recessions," there were no depressions, and the gross national product was on an unending upward curve. Business was booming, not just on paper as in 1929, but in terms of actual large increases in manufacturing plant size, production, foreign sales, new products, and so on.

Secondly, aircraft were gaining far greater utility. Twin-engine types like the Twin Bonanza came into the marketplace and found immediate acceptance. Giant strides were made in navigation and communication gear, which raised general aviation capabilities almost to the level of military and airline standards. As a matter of fact, modern general aviation aircraft often have equipment superior to that found in noncombat military aircraft.

Most important of all, the long-sought touchstone of commercial advantage began to occur. People were actually beginning to make money using airplanes. People in sales found that they could service larger territories better and faster and that the supply of parts to remote sites of industrial operations was increasingly important.

Coincident with this rising curve of aircraft utility, the rail system began to degrade. Commercial airlines were siphoning off the lucrative passenger traffic, and rail company management seemed to be too hidebound to compete. As a result, air transportation in all areas—airline, air cargo, and general aviation—began to be more competitive.

And the public's attitude toward air travel changed. As more and more people flew on airliners, the more natural it seemed to use general aviation aircraft for business. As profits and individual incomes soared through flying, it became increasingly possible to pay part (sometimes all) of the cost of an aircraft by charging it off to business and deducting it from taxes.

Aircraft manufacturers became much more sensitive to the public's demand and produced specialized types to meet the new requirements. Big concerns like Piper and Cessna began to blanket the marketplace with everything from two-place trainers to twin-engine executive aircraft. Beech provided a wide variety of high-performance aircraft that could almost match commercial airline block times over comparable distances.

Corporations soon perceived a need for privately owned aircraft that hadn't existed before—the need to multiply the effectiveness of their top executives time. In markets that had become intensely competitive, good executives were hard to find, and it was possible to get more utilization from someone who is not constrained by airline schedules. And the heady prospect of using the company plane was often inducement enough to retain the services of someone who might be able to get a higher salary elsewhere.

The first high-performance executive aircraft were often converted military planes—C-47s, B-25s, A-26s, B-24s, B-17s, and the like. The most important type was the twin-engine Lockheed Lodestar, which received super clean-up modifications first with Bill Lear in the Learstar and later from Howard in San Antonio, Texas. The operating costs of these aircraft were very high, of course, and, as they grew older, finding parts for their repair was increasingly difficult. In addition, many were not really comfortable, as the conversion from military to civil use, expensive as it was, couldn't alter the fundamental size and shape of passenger compartments. As the number of people flying in general aviation types grew, so did the number of civil types available to meet and exceed the performance of converted military aircraft.

Fortunately, year by year the amount of money to be made in general aviation grew. Part of this stemmed from a new breed of man in the field. Companies were no longer run by designers fascinated by flying and by airplanes, but by managers who recognized that making a profit and staying in business were more important than simply building a good airplane. Airplane companies diversified. They sought military contracts to complement their civil sales. And they even subcontracted for each other, an unheard-of practice before the war.

Even the very lowest people on the general aviation totem pole, the fixed-base operators who ran the airports and flying schools, began to prosper. One reason, of course, was the G.I. Bill, which provided a steady stream of subsidized students. More important in the long run was the new breed of business-oriented customer who could afford to rent or to buy and who could pay a reasonable (later an unreasonable) fee for hangar and tie-down spaces. The volume of repair work reached a point where decent equipment could be purchased and full-time mechanics employed. There was also an upswing in air taxi, photography, and other incidental means to make a buck.

The business plane breaks through

In the late 1950s, there occurred an almost revolutionary event, the coming of the business jet. Lockheed and North American made their basic military designs available for civil use: Lockheed's C-140 became the civil Jetstar, while the North American T-39 became the Sabreliner. By 1966, about one hundred of each had been sold to prestige-oriented, big-business customers.

But the spark that really ignited the jet age for business was the sleekly beautiful Learjet. Bill Lear announced to a laughing, unbelieving world that he was going to market a light, high-speed, low-cost executive jet. To everyone's amazement, it made its first flight on October 7, 1963, and, less than four years later despite the crash of the prototype, more than 130 were in service. The Jet Commander, by Aero Commander, was introduced about the same time as the Learjet, but its slightly higher price and less inspired looks didn't receive or earn the same degree of public attention. It lacked the "star quality" of the Learjet. Hence the Learjet revolutionized everyone's thinking about business transportation as a whole, not just about executive jets.

The tiny white Learjets offered something beyond mere luxurious private transportation and immense prestige. The aircraft was not more expensive than others; in fact, it cost about $600,000, only about 70 percent as much as the Lockheed or North American aircraft of the time. Rather, the Learjet was so terribly "with it," so supremely right. It was immediately used as background scenery in plush car advertisements, in movies, in TV commercials, in every expression of "jet set" living. And it deserved the image, for it was an aircraft of high performance and great reliability. It was soon outselling its competitors handily, to the great delight and satisfaction of Bill Lear.

The world of executive jet travel suddenly had a new, almost unlimited ceiling. Instead of aspiring for a converted Lodestar, where the economics and the prestige were intangible, companies could now seek to have a Learjet as an expression of success and convenience—and they would pay. The psychological impact was almost incalculable. While the production of jet transports was extremely sensitive to world market conditions, their existence provided an "umbrella" under which an enormous growth of single- and twin-engine conventional aircraft could be nourished, along with an amazing proliferation of types, equipment, and special conversions.

So we have come back full circle to the burning question, "Why should you start flying?" In the next chapter we will look at general aviation today, from puddle jumpers to fan jets, and see what the psychological and monetary rewards can be for you.

General Aviation—
where it's at and
where it's going

Oddly enough, you may earn your private license without ever realizing the mammoth breadth of the general aviation scene today. People tend to look at flight schools with their Cessnas, agricultural operations with their AgCats, and perhaps air taxi services with their King Airs—and regard that limited outlook as general aviation. The fact is that general aviation is a key part of our national transportation system, and, as such, it does more to keep the wheels of business turning than even the commercial airlines. This strong statement is somewhat biased, of course, but it is still based on some amazing "gee-whiz" statistics that offer the new private pilot license holder—you—considerable food for thought.

There are some pretty good reasons for general aviation's relatively low visibility even among people who like flying. The annual budget of its principal advocate—General Aviation Manufacturers Association—is relatively low. Even though GAMA does an intelligent, aggressive job of selling general aviation, it simply does not have the bucks to compete with the brilliant advertising campaigns of the airlines. Consequently, most people get their first—and often their only—ride in a commercial air transport, while on television every day 747s fly endlessly into the sunset and Frank Borman amiably pumps up his ground crews. No wonder most people associate flying with airlines. The equipment matters too. The droop-snooted Concorde or the lofty-tailed DC-10 is undeniably more impressive than a single-engine general aviation airplane or even a beautiful Learjet.

Amazingly, however, the flying done by the general aviation fleet is extremely significant. Let's "gee-whiz" a bit:

- Of the almost 200,000 aircraft on the active register, 99 percent are listed as the general aviation type. The remaining 1 percent belong to the airlines. Two-thirds of the "GA" aircraft are owned by private individuals and one-third by businesses.

- Only about 600 of the nation's 14,000 airports are served by scheduled airlines. The rest, the vast majority, must depend only on general aviation aircraft for service. Of the airports served by the airlines, 50 big ones generate 70 percent of the passenger traffic, while most of the remaining 500-plus depend on one or two flights per day.

- While the airlines, with their undeniable speed and efficiency, carry more than 250 million passengers a year from one major destination to another, the general aviation fleet carries an amazing 100 million people annually, primarily to airports where private planes can be used more conveniently than airlines.

None of these facts means that the airlines are less important. They simply point out the tremendous and vital segment of the nation's economy served by GA aircraft, as well as the potential market for the flier who wishes to progress from a beginner to a professional. The GA fleet could never replace the airlines in terms of passenger miles flown, particularly on the long-distance routes, nor does it wish to do so. It seeks only its place in the sun.

These facts might, perhaps, make you realize the importance of actively exploring all the possible job opportunities, in the air and on the ground, generated by this flood of short-haul activity going on all over the country. An enormous number of jobs are waiting—it just takes a little effort to look.

Where the jobs are

At present about three-quarters of a million pilots are in the United States, all presumably ready to fly the two hundred thousand active aircraft. At first glance, this ratio of pilots to planes seems to indicate that the only openings are for third pilot on a four-place airplane. Fortunately for you, the green bean, most of these pilots are not very active, and a significant percentage do no flying whatever, retaining their certificates as a purely sentimental gesture. Also, of the 250,000 people who hold commercial or air transport ratings, many don't do much flying but, like the others, nostalgically hold onto a treasured reminder of more exciting days in the past. And, sadly for old trouts like myself, many of the 250,000 are approaching the retirement age. A great percentage of this group learned to fly either in World War II (the "big war," they'll tell you) or shortly thereafter as a result of the G.I. Bill. Now they are moving slowly but inevitably to the sidelines.

As a result, the general aviation scene is more promising than it has been in years for the new pilots. Unfortunately, part of the promise is wrapped in the unvaryingly hard requirement to obtain more flying time so that you can move on to higher ratings. If you intend to fly for a living, you must ultimately get an instrument rating, a commercial rating, and, if you are really committed, eventually perhaps an air transport rating. In addition, you will undoubtedly wish to add to your skills by obtaining certificates to fly multi-engine aircraft, sea planes, and perhaps even helicopters. So the quest for employment is a multi-step affair. First you have to find employment that will permit you to use your private license while building time and taking instruction to get higher ratings, and then you'll have to seek employment to use your new licenses profitably.

"Quest" is a good word, for it implies a pilgrimage of sorts with the attendant privation, surprises, and odd disaster. With only a private certificate and a limited amount of flying time, you tilt with hundreds of others for a chance at the bottom of the totem pole. Don't despair, for it's the same in every worthwhile profession.

Business flying

The biggest slice of the general aviation pie is one that often goes unnoticed: business flying, the movement of key executives, products, supplies, or spare parts for the sole purpose of making a profit. "Sole purpose" may be a bit strong; many business planes are operated primarily either because top management wants the luxury and the prestige or because the top manager is a pilot and finds that having a company plane is a good way to maintain proficiency. In general, however, business aircraft have to pass the same sort of productivity analysis as any company tool: Does it contribute to the net profit of the company?

Most companies determine that an aircraft offers a return on investment that far exceeds the cost, especially when tax considerations are fully explored. Beech Aircraft Corporation, as do almost all manufacturing companies, puts out conservatively stated brochures that show exactly how an aircraft can save on taxes. In a typical example, a $120,000 Beech Duchess twin-engine airplane can return $75,000 of its cost over a five-year period, *without considering the utility of the aircraft in terms of saving executive time and without incorporating a realistic estimate of the real sale price of the airplane at the end of the five-year period.* (See the end of the chapter for the figures.) While the cost figures are important in persuading the board of directors to buy the aircraft, the real *raison de-être* of a business plane is to save executives' time—in effect to multiply their availability by shielding them from airline schedules and terminal delays.

Aha, you may say, if the average single-engine executive plane cruises at less than 200 mph and if the average airliner is almost three times faster, how can an executive plane save time? The answer, of course, is in the total control that a company can (and must, if it is to be efficient) exercise over the availability of the aircraft. In some instances—on trips from New York to San Francisco, for example—the airline usually wins hands down. But if the trip is of a shorter distance and particularly if it involves travel to airports not served by the major airlines, the corporate aircraft is a more efficient mode. On shorter trips, even between large cities, the general aviation aircraft can slip into city-center airports and save all the time associated with getting to the terminal, collecting baggage, racing like O. J. Simpson to rent a car, and then fighting the airport traffic into the city. Throughout vast areas in this great country you can get airline service in or out of an airport only once a day. If you miss that flight or if it is fully booked, you simply have to wait.

And, although it is usually intimated by word of mouth rather than by advertising, there is another extraordinarily important reason for owning a corporate aircraft. You have an almost intoxicating psychological effect on a prospective customer when you announce that, "We'll send our Learjet for you." Strong men have been known to buckle at their knees and their wives to weep with joy at the prospect of a sleek white jet pulling up at the Euphora Springs airport and rolling out a red carpet for them. Only slightly less important psychologically, and perhaps far more telling in practical terms, is the rapid delivery of a badly needed spare part by a company plane.

All right, we've established that business flying is important. But how many jobs are involved?

Opportunities in business flying

In corporate flight departments, about 35,000 people are engaged in business flying—not very many, yet worth shooting for. To get

Figure 7-1. The Cessna Model 402C is an exciting new airplane that accomplishes increased payload with a lengthened bonded wet wing, eliminating rivets, minimizing drag, increasing aspect ratio and climbing tip tanks. It's a clean, pleasing design that is very efficient.
Courtesy: Cessna Aircraft Company

started, you might simply have to choose a company that has an extensive corporate fleet and then take any job you can get, whether it is associated with aviation or not. Once on the inside, you can learn who the principal players are, then worm and wheedle your way into the flying side. This approach takes time, but it is an avenue.

About 70,000 people are employed in the sales and service aspects of air commuter operations, flight training, maintenance, and other system support. Once again, the odds are against you if you are a complete outsider. So be willing to take on any task, from line boy to ticket clerk, just so you get to be on the inside. People soon recognize where your real interests are, and they will admire you for it.

Specialties

Some aviation specialties are even more difficult than business flying to enter as a beginner, partly because they are interesting and partly because they pay well for the hazards involved.

They also demand a high-level of skill, and there is a great deal of competition for them. But, if they appeal to you, try to get taken on in any capacity, build up your flying time, and attend one of the schools that trains pilots for this exacting work.

Over 25,000 people are employed in agricultural flying. (Please, never say "crop dusting," particularly if you are trying to get a job. "Crop dusting" is a term of the past, with unfortunate associations that are totally incompatible with today's modern industry.) Even fewer and more specialized are flying pipeline patrol, aerial mapping, pollution control, and so on. About 10,000 people are involved in these jobs, and they usually require not only flying skill but also knowledge in an associated discipline, such as forestry, petroleum, and the like.

Jobs with manufacturers

The companies that manufacture major general aviation aircraft components—complete airframes, engines, and so on—employ about 50,000 people, as do the companies that manufacture the subcomponents and accessories. Perhaps your best bet in joining the employed ranks within aviation is among these 100,000. It won't be a flying job, but it will be in a place that can lead to a flying job, among people who are flying-oriented.

Self-employment

Finally, the toughest nut of all is the group of 10,000 self-employed flight instructors and mechanics, who slug out a living under the most difficult competitive circumstances and who perform an inestimable service to the general aviation community. Most are found on tiny airports, and most stick with their profession because of a love of flying. If you are totally dedicated and self-reliant, and if you value freedom more than security, you can try to join them.

The real opportunity in flying

Despite the attractiveness of some of the 250,000 job opportunities we've just covered, the best opportunity in aviation lies with the individual who is smart enough to marry an active life in general aviation to his or her own primary business interests. The classic case for career enhancement by flying is, of course, the salesperson. If you've been a good salesperson, "know your territory," beat your quotas, and are keeping your boss happy, you may be pleased but still not peaked out. If, by adding a private pilot's certificate to your portfolio of skills, you are able to service a territory three times as large as before, you may surprise both your boss and yourself. You'll build flying time, and you'll be able to charge off the cost of the aircraft as a business expense. (With only a private pilot's certificate, you won't be able to fly passengers for hire or to haul cargo, but you are certainly allowed to fly yourself on your job. Later, as we'll see, you'll probably want to get a commercial certificate, but that's another chapter.)

I've been told by salespersons who fly that another intangible value to their aviation skills is almost impossible to measure, but it is perhaps even more important than their increased mobility. They feel that customers place a great deal more credibility in a salesperson who flies; it's a psychological value, of course, but something about the earnest, serious nature of flying adds weight and authenticity to the salesperson's remarks. It's as if the potential customer is a little bemused that someone actually flew in to try to sell something, and, having done so, it must make the product worthwhile. Perhaps it's the self-confidence that flying engenders in pilots, or perhaps it's just America's love affair with aviation, but it is reflected in sales figures.

Other, less obvious careers are enhanced by a private pilot's certificate and the travel freedom it gives. Commercial exhibit designers for industrial trade shows, museums, and so on, work a hectic schedule in a business that requires continuous supervision to make a profit. Clients are usually hundreds of miles away, often in cities where airline service is marginal. Characteristically, changes in design and production requirements come up almost to the very minute the show opens. The ability to climb into your own plane, with a portfolio of sketches, without regard to airline schedules, and fly directly to where the decision must be made can lift you directly from the sketching board to the board room.

Engineers can also expand their capabilities with a private pilot's certificate that enables them to fly to field sites where they are needed. New factories, oil fields, mines, dam sites, and the like are all characteristically in the "boonies," away from the seventy or so airports where most airliners go. The corporate plane can even, if necessary, land in a pasture, although the airport is better practice. The point is that millions of dollars of capital equipment can be tied up unless the right person is on the spot to make a decision.

Immediacy is terribly important in most businesses, and there is no better communication than face to face. And, most often, there is a direct dollar saving, for if you have to take two or more people to a meeting, the direct costs of operations are usually less than the air fare.

Thousands of similar opportunities are waiting for people who don't settle for just being pilots, but instead combine their flying to an equally important career. It's important to note that this combination of skill seems to be synergistic; flying improves your chosen career chances, and advancement in your career improves your chances to fly. There are a number of reasons for this mutual benefit. First of all, you become more effective with the use of your time, so your productivity is higher. Second, flying an airplane is a serious, analytical business, and you apply the same techniques to your business. Third—and again psychology raises its head—you have more credibility with your co-workers and your clients if you are a pilot. This is particularly true if you fly your clients to the work sites (as a courtesy, no charge). They place their lives in your hands for the duration of that flight, and they do it again on the trip back. In between, at the site where the decisions are made, they're disposed to regard your remarks with care and attention.

Jobs—no, fun—yes: the private pilot as a star

Maybe you really don't want to fly as a part of your profession, and perhaps you have no desire to earn any advanced ratings. You can still fly proficiently and professionally—and have a world of fun— *if* you are rigorous enough with yourself as a private pilot. Remember, general aviation has no room for pilots who don't take flying and themselves seriously and who don't stay proficient.

Flying in the United States, you may take free advantage of some of the best facilities in the world. The private pilot's world benefits enormously from the government's tremendous investments in airports, navigation facilities, communications, and weather services. While these are intended primarily for the airlines' use, they are equally available to the private pilot who knows how to use them. With billions of dollars spent to create a safe, radar-controlled environment, private pilots, subject to the limitations of their certificates and their own capability, can take full advantage of them. Yet that sort of statement usually gives rise to a raging chorus on one side, reminding me that much remains to be done to ensure safety; in the other ear, an equally vocal outcry tells me that there are already far too many regulations. Let's just stop and consider a few questions: How much has been done? How many flights are made safely? And how determined are both business and government to improve flying facilities and safety in the future?

Is flying still fun despite government or because of it?

No other country in the world offers such a vast range of services (everything from printed material by the Government Printing Office to full-scale emergency Search and Rescue missions) to such an enormous number of pilots and aircraft, with no *direct* interference with personal rights. Certainly, increased regulations have forced pilots to buy certain equipment and to operate within certain designated high-density traffic areas with much greater regard for control. But none of these limitations stem from a governmental desire to create revenues or to suppress liberty; they arise from a need to enhance safety. The measures taken so far may not have been the best possible, but considering the size of the problem and the fact that solutions must in all countries be reached by a bureaucratic process, it has been a good effort.

So despite the flap in the press, the private pilot can still have fun flying. Fixed-base operators, far smarter now than in the past, cater to private pilots, seeing that they get fueled in short order, provided with a place to refresh themselves, and given every courtesy with regard to briefings, transportation into town, and so on. Where a cross-country trip used to be a little tedious, with even such rudimentary amenities as bathrooms hard to come by, you can now find more comfort at a little airport than at a highway rest area.

Even better, resorts are beginning to cater to private pilots, luring them to vacation at Treasure Bay in the Bahamas, at Maui in Hawaii, Yosemite, Mexico—sun and laughter are everywhere. The resort owners see that airports are maintained, custom officers available, and service up to U.S. standards. Flying doesn't make a vacation cheaper, but you can build up your flying time for about the same cost as airline tickets.

Flying on your vacations has additional advantages—and a few disadvantages. Like the business flier, you aren't tied to a schedule, and you don't lose time waiting around terminals. Weather becomes critically important, however, for you can get "weathered" out of or into a vacation, and sometimes you can do nothing but stop, park the airplane, and continue by surface. When this happens, you are, of course, committed to coming back for the airplane, with the additional attendant expense. But if you are careful and plot the weather carefully, chances are a flying vacation will be nothing but pleasure.

There are also an endless number of fly-ins, conventions, air shows, and the like to attend, almost every day of the month, all year long. No matter what your interests are—hobbies like soaring, whale-watching (honest!), antique aircraft, war birds, business planes, or professional meetings of the National Air Transport Association of the General Aviation Maintenance Groups—you are welcome to fly in to a relevant convention somewhere. When you do, you'll find yourself in an entirely different milieu from the person who drives to the party. You are on the inside, with special parking, identification, parties, and other benefits. It is part of the good life that can very rapidly spoil you for *not flying*.

Threats on the horizon

All is not calm in the world of general aviation, for two significant and perhaps terminal threats are coming up on the horizon. The first and perhaps most pressing threatens every section of the economy: the energy shortage. The second consists of legislation, for the General Aviation accident record, coupled with some near misses and tragic mid-air collisions, has created a crisis environment that may result in a severe curtailment of GA activity.

Energy

The whole country is gripped by a situation brought about by our own wastefulness, an unfortunate geographic and political disposition of liquid fossil fuels, and an economy geared precariously to the relentless consumption of gas and oil. General aviation is a part of this situation—a particularly threatened part, for a combination of a severe fuel shortage and a series of price hikes could well spell the end of flying as we know it today.

The most remarkable statistic that comes to hand is the relatively small amount of fuel used by general aviation—only 0.4 percent of all types of gasoline consumed in the U.S. and only about 4.5 percent of all U.S. jet fuel. In broader terms, refinery yields of liquid petroleum products break down into roughly the following percentages:

	%
Motor gasoline	43.9
Middle distillates	22.3
"Other" distillates	15.3
Residual fuel	11.5
Kerosene-type jet fuel	4.5
Naptha-type jet fuel	2.2
Aviation gasoline	.3
	100.0

Of the aviation gasoline, general aviation uses 78 percent, the military 15 percent, the airlines 6 percent, and "all other" 1 percent. The distribution of kerosene-type jet fuel is just the opposite: the airlines use 86 percent, the military 6.8 percent, general aviation 4.7 percent, and "all other" 2.5 percent.

Despite the small percentage of fuel it uses, general aviation is vulnerable because it seems to be a luxury activity. Certainly pleasure flying can be curtailed; the world won't end if you can't shoot touch-and-go landings or do loops and rolls. Yet pure pleasure flying is only 5 percent of the total aviation picture.

Severely curtailing business flying would have a monumental domino effect on the U.S. economy. Currently, the general aviation sector manufactures about 18,000 aircraft a year, with a total billing of nearly $1.7 billion dollars. Behind this sector are the hundreds of component and subcomponent manufacturers, airports, fixed-base operators, and so on. The arbitrary reduction or rationing of fuel in the general aviation sector could certainly add to the possibility of a general depression.

More probable than rationing is a continuing increase in fuel prices, for politicians find it easy to let prices—and presumably oil profits—go up, especially when it is cloaked in the guise of "providing incentives for oil exploration." You can rather easily estimate how much increases in fuel costs affect your pocketbook. The average general aviation aircraft burns about 10 gallons per hour. So for every 10-cent increase in the per-gallon price of gas, the cost of flying goes up $1. With a 50-cent increase in gas prices, there will be a $5 increase of cost per hour. If you are renting, the Cessna 152 that costs you $22 per hour today will cost you $27 tomorrow. Everyone who flies—military, airliner, and private—recognizes the deadly potential of the energy shortage.

Solutions? A number of steps are underway to mitigate the problem. Aircraft are now being flown at more economical cruise settings, sacrificing a little time en route to save a few gallons. The savings make a big difference to the airlines, and they help even private owners if they are conscientious.

Careful flight planning is another help. A straight line may not always be the most fuel-efficient route between two points if you can choose a route that has a tail-wind component. Even planning your flights to carry a minimum amount of fuel at a safe minimum can add a few miles per trip (not miles per gallon) to your statistics.

In the last analysis, however, the burden on improved fuel consumption lies squarely on consumers who demand that engine and airframe manufacturers depart from conventional practice to achieve better economy. Airplanes have to become smaller, lighter, and cleaner. Businesspilots have to realize that it is better to have a two- or three-place aircraft and occasionally leave someone at home than have a four-place aircraft and fly with three empty seats.

If consumers don't demand more fuel-efficient aircraft, then Congress will. If Congress doesn't, the problem could get out of control, and hundreds of airports across the country could become instant museums, flooded with aircraft too expensive to fly.

Legislation—safety or tyranny

Congress has already responded to problems with air safety. The tragic mid-air collision in San Diego between a light aircraft and the Pacific Southwest Airways Boeing 727 precipitated immediate legislation restricting the altitudes and airspaces in which certain general aviation aircraft could fly. Worse, this legislation may reflect only the tip of the iceberg, for a large body of public and private opinion favors the assurance of airline safety regardless of the resultant restrictions on general aviation.

Naturally, general aviation proponents react in just the opposite manner, citing cogent arguments for relaxing regulations and providing better facilities for general aviation aircraft. This view is almost bound to prevail, if sufficient consideration can be given to financing what needs to be done before the next major accident. If another tragedy like the one in San Diego occurs, a resultant rash of legislation could cripple general aviation forever.

Otherwise a whole series of programs could both improve the safety of the airlines and enhance general aviation's future. The principal aim of these programs would be to create landing field and airport facilities strictly for the general aviation aircraft, away from airline terminal areas. These would be costly to the taxpayer and to many of the businesses currently on existing airports. On the other hand, a systematic attempt at building the airfields, transportation facilities, and associated requirements of a general aviation airport system might well prove to be a tonic to the economy, ultimately paying for itself.

Notes on chapter seven   Although most people don't fall into the bracket where they can write off the ownership of a twin-engine aircraft for tax purposes, many businesses do. In fact, sales of modern executive aircraft hinge largely on this fact.

Beech Aircraft Corporation does everything well, and they provide you with very neat pamphlets that illustrate just how economical owning an aircraft can be. Following is an example of how ownership of a Beechcraft Duchess 76, a lovely twin-piston engine aircraft, can reduce a business' income tax expense:

> The tax benefits of ownership directly reduce the cost of your airplane. To illustrate how, let's assume (1) that your taxable income is subject to a 52-percent tax rate (federal and state), (2) that you purchase this airplane for $119,500 (which includes average optional equipment), and (3) that you elect to depreciate the airplane over five years on the double-declining-balance method.

Year	Depreciable Base	Depreciable Rate	Depreciation Expense	Tax Savings
1	$119,500	40%	$ 47,800	$24,856
2	71,700	40%	28,680	14,914
3	43,020	40%	17,208	8,948
4	25,812	40%	10,325	5,369
5	15,487	40%	6,195	3,221
Totals			$110,208	$57,308

Depreciation allowance for tax purposes should be determined after consultation with your financial adviser.

Purchase price of Duchess 76		$119,500
Less: Investment tax credit (6 2/3%)	$ 7,971	
Tax savings on depreciation	$57,308	65,279
Cost after five years		54,221
Less selling price of airplane (Residual Book Value)		9,292
$9,292—assumed to equal market for illustration purposes)		
Cost of airplane after tax savings		$ 44,929
Savings of time and costs resulting from ownership	$100,000	
Less 52% of above	$ 52,000	
After-tax savings from ownership		48,000
Less cost of airplane after tax savings		44,929
Savings brought about by ownership (after tax)		$ 3,071

Note: A larger part of the savings occurs in the first years of ownership because of the tax advantage in those years. Your tax adviser may suggest other options to fit your situation, which will lower your cost even more. A seven-year depreciable life, for instance, allows the full 10-percent investment tax credit, reducing the $44,929 to $40,950, and an adviser may recommend switching to a straight-line method after a few years for a lower residual value.

The figures are really conservative, particularly the selling price of the airplane, which is more likely to be $75,000 than $9,292.

Courtesy Beech Aircraft Corporation

Onward and Upward—Time and The Rating Game

The decision to fly for a living is like a decision to marry, to enter the priesthood, or to go to medical school, for it involves the prospect of several years of effort, hard work, low wages, and utter satisfaction. Once you've got your private license and have that fire burning in your belly to become an airline pilot, you will have to acquire lots of flying time—an expensive process—and a series of ratings from the FAA. With the best of luck, you'll pick up your flying time in the kinds of jobs we'll be talking about later. The ratings will require additional schooling, along with a great deal of effort and skill on your part. Before investigating all the costs in terms of time and money, let's see what the ratings offer you.

First of all, they permit you to fly for hire. Unless you have a commercial license, there is no way for you to use an airplane for anything except your personal business or pleasure.

Second and more important, acquiring the time and the ratings inevitably makes you a better, safer pilot. The training, while in some ways mildly repetitive of that you received while getting a private license, is in fact much more rigorous and demanding. Your relationship with your flight instructor is far different; he or she expects you to try very hard and to perform with competence. This time the instructor is far less forgiving of any little lapses of memory or errors in judgment, for the acquisition of a new rating is also a license to intrude on the lives of others. People who hire you to fly them someplace expect that your instructors and flight check pilots have done their jobs thoroughly.

Prospective employers look, beyond the ratings, at your skills; having the certificate isn't enough. You have to demonstrate not only a proficiency in getting from point A to point B, but also an awareness of the operating economics of flying, a consciousness for safety of personnel and equipment, and a positive attitude that flying is a business as well as a romance.

It may be a poor comparison in academic terms, but, in terms of attitude, advanced ratings are graduate degrees. You've declared your intention to become a professional pilot, and, as a candidate, you are supposed to behave like candidates behave for advanced degrees. In other words, schooling isn't just something to run through so that you can pass exams; it means that you consciously become part of the aviation scene, soaking up the literature, being around when needed, listening mostly, talking only when you have something to say. Flying, intoxicating as it may be as a sport, is affected by legislative, environmental, and social conditions, and an intelligent professional pilot is aware of these interactions. There are committees to join, societies to belong to, and friends to make if you want to really capitalize on the opportunities that advanced ratings offer. Let's get started!

The 200-hour drive

Until the "regs" are changed, you'll have to acquire either 200 hours for an instrument rating or 250 hours to obtain a commercial certificate. If you've logged 50 hours in the process of obtaining your private certificate, you have 150 hours to go, just for openers. How do you get them?

If you are wealthy, you can just pay for them—shell out the necessary money to rent the airplanes, with the odd instructional hour thrown in as you progress. If you have this kind of money, you don't need any advice from me or anybody else.

If you have to make your dollars stretch, there are a number of ways to go about it. The best way, of course, is to seek employment, in any capacity, with a fixed-base operator; try to convince the owner that you can be a useful back-up pilot on trips that don't have a full passenger load. You'll at least be able to log co-pilot time—some of which counts for your advanced ratings. And if the FBO is a nice guy, he'll let you log some first pilot time and, if a real pro, let you shoot a landing or two.

If a job isn't possible, you can usually find someone to team up with to share the rental costs and the time. Sharing permits you to fly more often, even if you log only half as much first pilot time. It's amazing what you can learn from watching another person fly, for you learn not only what to do—but what not to do. A flying club is worthwhile in this approach. The cost of flying is moderately lower, but, more important, you log your time under some sort of generalized supervision and have benefits of good maintenance, flying safety meetings, and so on.

This rough little period between 50 and 200 hours is the most trying—and dangerous—time in a young pilot's life. It's trying because it's hard to keep your enthusiasm up, much less your proficiency, when you have to squeeze in your flying at a rate of an hour a week. It's dangerous because your confidence and your ability are on divergent curves. You think you're better than you are, and, through lack of practice, you inevitably begin to lose your sharpness. Your sense of commitment must prevail; if you are determined to make a career of flying, you'll surmount the problems of this period and be ready to earn your advanced "degrees." If you are not committed, you'll drift away, and it's just as well.

Instrument rating and commercial pilot's certificate

The FARs spell out in sometimes tedious length all the requirements to earn each rating, and brief excerpts of these requirements are printed at the end of the chapter. Essentially, however, you can earn a commercial license with a minimum of 250 hours of flying time, broken down into certain specified sorts of training. Practically speaking, it's almost impossible to get exactly the right break-out with only 250 hours; too many things intervene, including such distasteful events as failed flight checks, prohibitive weather, and so on. It really doesn't matter, the 250 hours is a regulatory minimum, and if you acquire 300 hours before you take your check, it's probably to your advantage.

One of the primary stepping stones to your commercial certificate is the acquisition of an instrument rating, which has its own set of minimum requirements. You can get what is essentially a "limited" commercial certificate without an instrument rating. It carries a restriction prohibiting you from carrying passengers at night or for hiring out on a cross-country trip of more than 50 miles. This limitation obviously counters your aspirations unless you have a very special situation. Besides, your safety is enhanced immeasurably if you have the capabilities derived from instrument training.

The full instrument rating, perhaps more than any other, requires special skills and judgment. Unless you are proficient in instrument flight, you are in deadly peril when flying under instrument conditions. And although this sounds like a truism, every year noninstrument-rated pilots find themselves flying either into clouds or the ground under them, with catastrophic results.

Every pilot is probably guilty of occasionally flying in an

incredibly sloppy manner under visual flight rules and surviving without any problem. You'll let your attention wander, drift into a warning area, forget to switch tanks and the engine quits, start a takeoff roll with the mixture in lean, or make any one of a number of goofs that can be rectified and even glossed over. Many a pilot has forgotten to put the gear down until the warning horn blew and has only a momentary private embarrassment from it.

But flying poorly under instrument conditions is an entirely different matter. The difficulty arises from the fact that your body, on good old Mother Earth, is perfectly adapted to maintaining its equilibrium by responding to long-trusted inputs from your eyes, your sense of touch, and from special motion-sensing organs in your inner ear. These sensory inputs have been reinforced by years of experience with visual clues. You expect the earth to be beneath your feet, separated from the sky above by a well-defined horizon. You associate this basic orientation with your kinesthetic or postural sense: You have long since grown used to your feet being planted firmly on the ground, with one "G" of gravity holding you there.

Only rarely do these routine signals become disrupted, usually as a result of some sort of game or carnival ride. Have you ever had a tough two minutes on a "Wild Whipper," one of those nauseating rides that sling you around like a bucket of water, letting centrifugal force scramble your sense organs and the ill-advised hot dog at the same time? Some people are particularly susceptible to this and other forms of motion sickness, as evidenced by the big sales of Dramamine and other similar remedies. No matter how susceptible you are to this sort of sensory disruption, on the ground it doesn't matter very much; down remains down, and a friendly hand can guide you to a place to rest until the problem goes away.

Instrument flight is entirely different. Although motion sickness may not be the difficulty, disorientation may be, and this can be everything from disconcerting to fatal. The essential difference, of course, is that your body still receives signals, but they may be erroneous. The sensations that gravity induces in your body can be perfectly simulated by the centrifugal force resulting from a turn. Similarly, the signals generated by the equilibratory organs of your inner ear can become completely false. Worst of all, there are no exterior visual clues to set things right. The horizon is masked by the clouds or the night, and your only reliable guide to up or down or left and right are the instruments before you.

Sometimes it's not what the clouds hide that confuses; you

may get completely false information from what you see. An angled line of darker clouds can appear very much like the horizon line, and you can feel absolutely driven to bank the airplane so that it is aligned with the clouds. On a dark night, the scattered lights of towns below can merge with the twinkle of stars so that there is no longer any up or down, but simply a universe of pinpoints of light.

Your postural senses fare no better; under normal conditions on the ground, or in flight, gravity exerts its spell on your equilibrium by means of a one "G" vector from the top of your head straight to the center of the earth. Yet if you make a turn under instrument conditions, accidently or on purpose, the effect of centrifugal force can shift that vector so that it points at an angle. And the "seat of your pants," the oh-so-fallible guide to the pioneers, tells you one thing while the instruments tell you another.

The most treacherous sensations of all, however, derive from erroneous signals from the tiny organs of the vestibular mechanism in your inner ears (Figure 8-1). These little chaps, so dependable on the ground, are unable to detect the effects of centrifugal force in the air. Like the postural senses, they too are fooled, but they are also flummoxed by the effect of turns and by acceleration and deceleration. This actual mechanism is extraordinarily sophisticated, but it can be explained in simplistic terms. Essentially, fluid moves in three canals, each of which is oriented in separate planes at 90° to the other. Tiny "hairs" inside the canals, wafted by the movement of the fluid, communicate the effect of the movement to your brain. On the ground, the movement of the fluid is caused by ordinary body motions, turning your head, and so on, and all the signals so generated can easily be interrupted.

Once again a child's game can serve as an example. Remember how kids close their eyes, and then whirl around and around so that they can't walk a straight line? They've set the fluid in motion in the inner ear and respond dizzily to its garbled signals until visual and kinesthetic clues sort everything out again.

Under visual flight conditions, your body experiences the same physical sensations as it does under instrument conditions. The fluid in your vestibular mechanism is displaced, centrifugal force simulates gravitational direction, and so on. But your eyes constantly provide visual information that permits your mind to overcome the false stimuli coming in, and it does so well that you are only rarely, if ever, conscious of any conflict.

During instrumented flight, however, centrifugal force and the

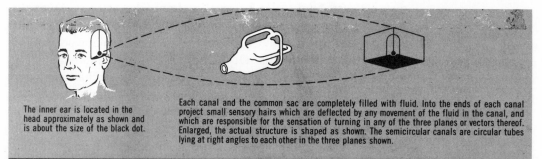

The inner ear is located in the head approximately as shown and is about the size of the black dot.

Each canal and the common sac are completely filled with fluid. Into the ends of each canal project small sensory hairs which are deflected by any movement of the fluid in the canal, and which are responsible for the sensation of turning in any of the three planes or vectors thereof. Enlarged, the actual structure is shaped as shown. The semicircular canals are circular tubes lying at right angles to each other in the three planes shown.

MECHANICS OF THE INNER EAR

As the head is rotated, the canal in that plane of rotation will move with respect to the fluid in it. Since this fluid has inertia, the resulting deflection of the sensory hairs will cause a sensation of turning.

SENSATION OF MOVEMENT TO BRAIN

NO ROTATION

NO SENSATION—Fluid accelerated to same speed as canal—(No deflection).

The static organ is located in the bottom part of the common sac, and consists of delicate sensory hairs projecting upward, on which rest small crystals of chalk.

MOVEMENT

SENSATION OF TURNING to brain. Rotation of canal deflects hairs.

SENSATION of turn in opposite direction. Rotation stopped deflects hairs in opposite direction.

The load borne by these sensory hairs changes in the head with every change of the head with respect to gravity, and this creates the sensation of tilting the head or body.

SEMI-CIRCULAR CANALS CAN PRODUCE FALSE SENSATIONS

IN A SLOW STEADY TURN YOUR SEMICIRCULAR CANALS CAN FOOL YOU

Straight flight

Beginning of turn. Only canals move.

Continuing turn fluid begins to move.

Still in turn fluid catches up with walls. Illusion created.

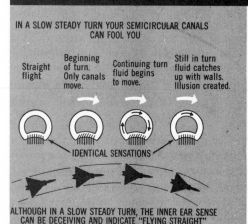

IDENTICAL SENSATIONS

ALTHOUGH IN A SLOW STEADY TURN, THE INNER EAR SENSE CAN BE DECEIVING AND INDICATE "FLYING STRAIGHT"

WHEN YOU STOP TURNING, YOUR SEMICIRCULAR CANALS CAN FOOL YOU

Start of right turn. Canal moves. Fluid stationary.

Continuing turn. Fluid catches up with walls.

Stopping turn. Canals stop. Fluid continues.

Beginning of left turn.

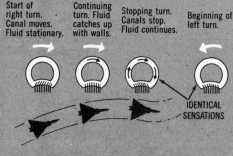

IDENTICAL SENSATIONS

ALTHOUGH THE TURN HAS BEEN STOPPED, THE INNER EAR CAN BE DECEIVING AND INDICATE A "LEFT TURN"

Figure 8-1.   Working of the inner ear and its effect on pilots.
Source: Air Force Manual 51-37, Instrument Flying.

effect of acceleration and deceleration can cause motion in the fluid which transmits entirely erroneous signals. You must therefore learn—and sometimes force yourself—to let the information on the instrument panel substitute for ordinary visual clues, to perform the function of a bright blue sky and a well-defined horizon in orienting you correctly. This technique is a little easier said than done, for you have to overcome years of utter reliance on inner signals and transfer this faith to a series of round dials. At the same time, you must continue to fly the airplane, monitor the radio, and maintain a serene air of confidence for any fellow pilots or passengers.

Only good instrument training and continuous practice permit you to do so. If you are well-trained in instrument flight, know your procedures, and have a well-equipped aircraft, you are safe as—and some maintain even safer than—flying under ordinary visual conditions.

Learning to fly instruments

Once you have the appropriate assortment of hours and have plunked down your $1,800 for the course, what can you expect? Typically, you'll be flying a Cessna 172 or the equivalent for 25 to 30 hours, perhaps a tad more if you are a little slow in some areas. But before you get into the airplane, you'll receive 60 hours of classroom instruction, heavily slanted towards instrument procedures, FAA written exam material, and, once again, weather. Because so much instrument flying is dependent on the clear, precise use of radios, you'll have lots of lab work simulating all the calls that you'll make or receive in flight. Radio training is invaluable, for the classic argot of controllers becomes even more clipped and precise during times of heavy weather traffic, and if you are unfamiliar with the jargon you'll lose precious time.

The expense and difficulty in obtaining the 200-hour flying time prerequisite has generated some strong sentiment for making it possible to begin working on an instrument ticket right after getting your private license. This is, after all, the general method of instruction used by the military services, and it makes sense for a number of reasons. First of all, it introduces the new pilot into the rigors—and benefits—of instrument flight soon after completing the private pilot's course. The candidate is still sharp and fresh. Second, it offers an enormous operating economy, for the hours poured into instrument training would count in the pursuit of the commercial license.

Both the commercial and instrument license requirements allow for the use of simulator training in lieu of actual flight time. A far cry from the old "Blue Box" classic Link trainer, modern simulators are worth every cent invested in them both by the fixed-base operators who own them and the students who rent them. The typical instrument training course calls for 10 or 11 hours in the simulator, and this amount of time is usually enough, although you can choose to buy a little more time if you feel you need it to smooth out any problems you might be having in the air. The commercial license permits up to 50 hours simulator time to be counted, while the instrument license permits up to 40 hours.

Simulators are in many ways even better than actual flight training, for you lose no time getting to or from a practice area, and, of course, you can never be weathered out of a scheduled session. The feeling of flight is not entirely duplicated, but you'd be surprised at how close even the relatively inexpensive simulators used by general aviation come to being the real thing. The more absorbed you are in the lesson—an instrument let-down, for example—the more real it seems to you. The overwhelming advantage of simulators, of course, is that you can make mistakes—even lethal ones—and learn from them without danger. Working with a competent instructor, the simulator is especially valuable in teaching you procedures, radio calls, and so on. As valuable as simulator training is in general aviation, it has become absolutely indispensable in commercial and military applications, where operating costs and the energy shortage preclude practice flights in real airplanes.

During the flight portion of your instrument flight training, you'll learn once again that *all* flight maneuvers are combinations of the four basic flight elements—climbs, dives, straight and level flight, and turns. The principal difference, of course, is that in instrument flight you no longer have the outside horizon as a point of reference. Instead you must depend on those little round dials set into the instrument panel. Nonetheless, instrument flying calls for a very precise technique, one that depends on a smooth light touch and on the ability to divide your attention among a number of important stimuli.

The attitude indicator is the instrument you look at most often, for it shows the attitude of the plane relative to the horizon. If the wings of the little plane on the instrument are level with the horizon, so are the wings of the real plane level with the real horizon. If the little plane's nose dips below the horizon, the same thing is happening in the real world.

But as graphic as the attitude indicator is, it provides only some of the clues you must absorb. The competent instrument pilot continuously scans the panel and cross-checks airspeed, headings, altitude, and vertical velocity, as well as the attitude indicator. With a little practice all these signals become integrated. If you sense a change in heading, you know that you must make a slight change in the attitude of the wings to correct for it. If you notice a slight climb on your vertical velocity indicator, you automatically compensate by lowering the nose, using the attitude indicator. As you learn to make more rapid cross-checks and to integrate information better, instrument flight becomes easier, for you tend to correct situations as they develop, and problems don't have time to build. The instructor won't demand that you progress faster than your ability allows, for his aim is to graduate you, not to wash you out. As complicated as it may sound, you'll soon acquire a practiced familiarity.

As your skill increases, you are introduced to the art of navigation by instruments. You'll be able to fly cross-country, never seeing the ground but unerringly moving from one point to your destination. Actual instrument flight is demanding but terribly rewarding: no sight is more beautiful than that of the runway lights when you break out from a cloud deck, right on course.

Don't let the skill and judgment requirements of instrument flight deter you. They are all well within the competence of the average pilot, *if* you practice conscientiously. Once again, however, if you don't intend to be a conscientious, professional pilot, your best bet is to look around for another hobby.

The commercial certificate

Once you've committed the time and energy to acquiring an instrument rating, it won't be difficult for you to acquire the additional time and skill necessary for the commercial certificate. The course will be expensive, however, for you'll be getting a lot of flying time in more than one type of airplane. A "plain vanilla" commercial course costs between $3,500 and $5,000, depending on the planes you choose to fly. If you have the money, you can save some time by acquiring a multi-engine rating at the same time—at about $1,500 extra.

For these large sums you'll get another 75 hours of classroom time, 25 hours of dual time in a Cessna 152 or Piper Tomahawk, 75 hours solo in the same plane, and then 10 to 12 hours of dual time in a larger, more sophisticated airplane with a constant-speed prop and retractable landing gear, possibly a Cessna Cardinal RG or a Piper Lancer.

These amounts tend to be minimums, and it's entirely possible that you might need some additional time practicing some elements before your instructor feels you are ready for your flight check. Don't begrudge these extra hours. Expensive as they might be, they'll pay you dividends throughout your career, for they are smoothing out rough spots when they should be smoothed—while you are still in training.

The essential elements of commercial pilot flight training are rigor and refinement. When you were learning to fly, a flight instructor allowed you some latitude in headings and altitudes if you were trending to the right flight path. Not so in the commercial course; your flight instructor calmly and consistently points out that you've departed from the desired airspeed by a couple of knots, that your altitude has drafted 30 feet off, or that your heading is not being maintained precisely. Commercial flight instructors are not interested in seeing you fly *near* the desired figures; they expect to see you flying *exactly* as prescribed.

Another facet of this advanced work is the integration of the whole flying environment into each flight. If, for example, you are practicing making short-field takeoffs and landings, the instructor expects you to use exactly the correct technique. But he also expects you to be aware of traffic in the area, possible changes in wind or weather, the amount of airwork you have remaining to do, and so on. This training does not include the spoon-fed arrangement of your private pilot's course. You are a certificated pilot, and the instructor expects you to fulfill the real world requirements. Thank God too, for you will be flying in the real world, where your safety and others depend on a wide-awake involved consciousness of the air around you.

Don't be distressed by the prospect of such thorough and rigorous evaluation, for the courses are designed to teach you what you need to know. Just maintain the skills you displayed in getting a private certificate and the serious desire to learn, and you will do well.

Once you've taken the instruction and passed the flight examination, you'll enter a competitive arena where a good many pilots seek a relatively limited number of jobs. Once again, your best bet is to be completely flexible as to salary, location, and working hours. You should also evidence a complete desire to please and an infinite capacity for praising the flying skills of the pilots whom you'll serve as second banana.

Flight instruction

Oddly enough, one of the most frequent routes to accumulating flying time is by obtaining yet another rating—that of certified flight instructor. You may become a teacher instead of a student. A natural upward mobility in the profession lures flight instructors with a thousand or more hours flying time into better paying, less demanding jobs as corporate pilots. As a result, there are always openings for instructor pilots, even relatively low-time recent graduates like yourself.

This state of affairs may seem to contradict what we have said before about seeking out experienced instructor pilots for your own instruction. Not really, for we are talking about the real world and about what you can do to survive as a pilot in it. If you begin instructing with perhaps 300 or 400 hours, you may not be the most experienced flight instructor on the line, but you may very well be the best motivated and the most sincere. If you wish to do as good a job of instructing as you did in learning, you can provide your students with a fine course of instruction. If, on the other hand, you are not totally dedicated and don't take all the extra steps in preparation, study, and so on, then you won't be a good instructor and your students will suffer. In this, as in everything to do with flying, the result is up to your own level of dedication.

In this real world, unfortunately, many individuals don't have your dedication, and, as a result, the problem of inadequate flight instruction plagues the industry. The situation provides you with a problem and an opportunity. The problem is to choose a good flight instructor, who is not contributing to the sentiment that the general aviation safety record is inexorably linked to poor flight instruction.

The opportunity is to become a good flight instructor yourself, one who transcends the ordinary considerations of working hours, salary, and one who has the determination to make sure the student learns everything possible in the short time available.

A flight instructor's course adds another $1,700 to $2,000 to your aviation dues. You'll receive 45 hours or so of classroom and tutorial instruction, plus about 25 hours instruction in a relatively sophisticated airplane, a Cessna Cardinal retractable-gear type, for example. If you wish to instruct in instrument flight, another $1,200 gains you 20 additional hours of tutored instruction, plus another 20 hours flying time.

When you receive your flight instructor rating, you will probably be able to get a job instructing as long as you have the right temperament for it and are willing to accept the relatively low wages for the privilege of building up hours. Instructors, with very rare exceptions, are paid on the basis of the number of hours flown. They are not paid for those essential hours of pre- and post-flight briefings, nor are they paid when weather, maintenance, or student no-shows keep them out of the air. The FAA limits instructors to eight hours of flying a day, and wisely so, for eight hours of instruction is a killing pace. Unfortunately, on many days instructors can't log any time, and on many more they can log only two or three hours. At an average hourly rate of $8, it's easy to see that you won't get rich quick instructing.

On the other hand, no one learns more from flight instruction than the flight instructor. Each hour spent with a student, exasperating or white-knuckled as it may be, is a learning experience that enhances the instructor's utility and ability. Best of all, the use of the aircraft and its fuel is free, and each hour logged is an hour closer to a job as a corporate pilot or with the airlines.

Airline transport pilot rating

If you go back and count up your expenses thus far, you reach something like $10,000 to $12,000 invested in instruction, plus other amounts in flying time, ground schools, equipment, and so on. You've invested a sizable figure, so why not go all the way to an ATR, an Airline Transport Pilot rating? The prerequisites are formidable: 1,500 pilot hours, a commercial license, an instrument rating, and, of course, a first-class medical certificate. Are the rewards worth it?

From a monetary sense, they certainly are. Airline captains, flying first-line equipment, earn as much as $80,000 to $100,000 a year, plus many tangible fringe benefits. Their prestige is great and the number of flying hours so limited that they actually have 18 to 20 days a month of free time. As a result, many own second businesses, more to fill in their free time than for extra income.

But this is only one side of the picture. These $100,000-a-year captains represent the tip of a pyramid of decades of effort. Behind them lie long hours as first officer, co-pilot, and flight engineers, of lay-offs and uncertainty, and of semi-annual flight physicals that can remove them instantly from flight status. They have achieved an invaluable level of skill and flying knowledge, and although any individual trip may be so routine as to be boring, they must be prepared to bring all their skill and knowledge to bear in the split second that an emergency develops. Just breaking into the industry is not easy, because the requirements for new pilots fluctuates with the fortunes of business. When profits are down, new job opportunities are few; when public demand for air transportation goes up, there is a sudden hiring flurry.

The training for an ATR is not as expensive as might be expected. For a multi-engine rating, you get about 70 hours of ground school instruction and 25 hours of dual flight time in a twin-engine plane like the Cessna 310, for $2,500 to $3,000. If you want a rating in a higher-powered type, or in a jet like the Learjet or Saberliner, the tuition goes up another $7,000 to $12,000. The training might be worth the money if you have a good shot at a corporate pilot's job; it's probably not if you are going to try to work your way into the airline system.

One of the most often asked questions about training of this nature is, "Does it really qualify me?" After all, 25 hours is not very much time in a twin-engine aircraft, and you receive your type rating in a Learjet after only 40 additional classroom hours and 17 hours in the airplane. The answer is yes and no. It doesn't qualify you to be a first pilot in the Learjet, but it does qualify you to be a copilot, from which position you learn enough to check out as first pilot.

You have to remember that all flight training is cumulative, and there is an enormous amount of skill transfer. The difference between a Cessna Cardinal and a Cessna 310 is not very much in terms of the actual flying. Once you have mastered the different techniques involved in jet flying, there is not an enormous gap between the 310 and the Learjet, in the way that either is flown. There are great differences in speed, of course, and your planning has to be of a different order, but you can probably fly a Learjet even more easily than you can a 310—when everything is going well.

The big difference, of course, is that larger, faster aircraft generally have more complicated systems and are more demanding of the pilot in emergency situations. So you must qualify as a co-pilot first: You learn, become familiar with the aircraft, and then gradually acquire the experience necessary before an owner entrusts a $1 million airplane and its important passengers to your care.

Let's assume that you have your ATR, have elected not to get a rating in one of the corporate jet aircraft, and are trying hard to get a job as an airline pilot. What are your prospects? In general, they are good if you are patient enough to make applications at several and then wait for the hiring needs to match your availability. For years, the airlines obtained most of their pilots from the military, and for years the military was training more than enough to supply its own needs. Now things are different, for military pilot training has been vastly cut down for reasons of economy. As a result the airlines are looking to general aviation pilots as a source. Airline pilot applicants usually face a buyer's market, and as a result airlines have been able to keep qualification standards high. A college degree, 20-20 vision, and as much as 1,000 hours flying time are usual requirements, although in times of pilot applicant shortage, some or all of these might be waived.

More important to you and your pocketbook, however, is the almost universal requirement that you earn a flight engineer's certificate. For a variety of reasons, some resulting from union pressures and some from practical necessity, most airlines require that prospective pilots begin their careers as flight engineers. This is undoubtedly a good idea from the standpoint of the knowledge that a pilot gains about an airplane's structure and systems when flying the "third seat." On the other hand, a flight engineer is somewhat like the prima donna's understudy—always straining for a chance to perform, and rarely getting it.

Because of the type of equipment involved, a flight engineer's rating for a large airliner like a Boeing 707 or 727 is much more expensive than even an airline transport pilot rating. Weeks of classroom training, plus 80 hours of cockpit precedural training, precede 30 hours in airline cockpit training. Following this, an arrangement is usually made with an airline to permit the student to have 20 hours of work in an actual flight simulator, half of which is spent in observing and half in actually operating the simulator. During these eight or nine weeks of training, students never leave the ground or even get into a real airliner, but they do become fully indoctrinated in all normal and emergency procedures to the point that they can pass an FAA flight check in an actual flight in 707 or 727.

The cost—up to $7,500!

As a flight engineer/pilot applicant, you still have plenty of competition, but the airlines are faced with a mandatory retirement age of 60, and time is on your side. The recent boom in recreational travel has begun to offset somewhat the decline in total number of aircraft operated by the airlines. So you have, at least in the near future, a reasonable chance of employment.

Military training

Let's analyze your meteoric rise from student pilot to ATR rating. It's taken several years and perhaps $20,000 in tuition fees. You've had to take low-paying jobs, work odd hours, be ready to move, and in general subordinate yourself to the whims of your employers— just to build up experience and that precious flying time. Is there a better way?

There is indeed, although many protest my point of view. The better way is to get your flight training from the military, determined to give good service while you are in and equally determined to get out and join the airlines as soon as you can. Many people don't like the idea of joining the Air Force or the Navy to learn to fly because they don't like the prospect of taking orders, moving around the country, and so on. The fact is that you'll probably have to take more orders and make more moves as general aviation pilot struggling to get your ratings. And you'll almost undoubtedly be paid less.

But the major consideration, the one that you should think about most of all if you are interested in being a professional pilot, is that the flight training from either the Air Force or the Navy is by far the best in the world. You fly the best equipment, receive the most stringent checks, and, in general, achieve far more in the five to seven years of military service than you could on your own.

There are, of course, drawbacks. The military is highly selective and demands a four-year college education and first-class physical condition. During a shooting war, you might be expected to do some shooting or, worse, to get shot at. (The terrible irony is, of course, that in the next war—God forbid that there be one—it will probably be safer to be in a combat airplane than in your own bedroom.)

Checking with your local Air Force and Navy recruiters and getting the full picture of your prospects won't cost you a cent. Pay is good while training, and competitive afterwards. You don't make as much as an airline pilot, but you sure make more than a flight instructor. You have a chance to fly a lot of different airplanes and see a lot of places you might never get to see otherwise. The U.S. Army also has a flight training program, but it is concerned more with helicopters and small fixed-wing aircraft. The qualifications for training are slightly different from either the Air Force or the Navy, and it might be suitable for you.

As formidable as the training and requirements sound, the skies are filled with greying men who went through the process and are now earning huge salaries flying with the airlines, reaping its rich rewards. If you really want to be an airline pilot, the paths are open—you simply have to want it bad enough.

What it costs versus what it pays

Earning advanced ratings and working yourself into a good flying job extract a cost in terms of tuition and in foregone opportunities. What can you expect to earn? The answer depends, of course, on your job, the type of equipment you are flying, and your geographic location.

Let's look at some extremes and a few of the means. As far as jobs are concerned, a captain on a Cessna 414 (a $300,000 twin-engine, eight-passenger airplane) makes an average of about $17,000 a year, whereas the chief pilot of an organization flying the Gulfstream II jet makes almost $50,000 a year. You can get an idea of the difference that the type of equipment makes when you know that the co-pilot on a Learjet makes about $18,000 a year, slightly more than the captain of the 414. In general, captains of business jets average about $30,000 per year, while captains of turboprop aircraft like the Gulfstream I or Mitsubishi MU-2 earn about $23,000. Down the scale, captains of piston-engine equipment average about

$19,000. Airline pilot salaries are, of course, much higher. As a result, the airlines act as a gigantic selection mechanism, pulling the best pilots from the pool of general aviation candidates in numbers that vary from year to year but with an appeal that never varies.

Airline pilots' pay is a controversial subject, and the public's awareness is heightened by the publicity given the high salaries during times of labor strife. During the spring of 1978, in a series of full-page advertisements in major newspapers, Northwest Orient Airlines trumpeted the fact that a captain of Northwest 747s made in excess of $105,000 per year; they also boasted the company's offer of an average increase in wages and benefits of over $30,000 in the next three years. Figures like that stupefy average, middle-class people trying to keep their income for a family of four out of the poverty level. It doesn't help to be reminded that the same Northwest captain was working an average of eleven days per month. These advertisements have two other effects: One is to anger everyone not making $105,000 a year, and the other is to inspire every young pilot to try and join the airlines.

Like all situations, there is more to it than this. Airline captains earn anywhere from $36,000 to $80,000 and more, depending on their seniority, equipment, and routes. A first officer, the elegant euphemism for co-pilot, can earn various sums from the miserable starting salary of $8,000 all the way to $53,000, on the average. A second officer (flight engineer) also starts at $8,000 but can average as much as $46,000 before graduating to co-pilot. (Just for the record, it's a sad comment on the airline policy that flight attendants—despite their unstinting services—make only from $9,000 to $17,000 per year.)

The moral of these numbers is obvious. If you are qualified, seek employment with the airlines *if top dollar is your goal*. The airlines have some drawbacks: They have a rigid seniority system that makes the military look slovenly, and flying a big airplane over the same route day after day, 95 percent of the time on autopilot, is not really very thrilling. A big compensation, of course, is that most airline pilots can afford to own their own planes, and an amazing percentage do.

With these salaries, you'd assume that a glut of pilots would be waiting to get into an airline slot. Though true in the past, several encouraging factors are at work for the aspirant pilot. The first is that more than 10,000 retirements are expected from airline pilot ranks in the next ten years. Coupled with an expected growth in airline aircraft numbers, this means that there will be between 15,000 and 20,000 openings in the next decade. At the same time, one of the major sources for airline pilots, the military, is no longer as fertile as it was. Pilot training costs have forced the services to curtail their pilot programs by about 75 percent. So despite the fact that internal dissatisfaction with military flying (too few flight hours, too low pay, too slow promotions) makes more people wish to leave, there are simply fewer pilots available to draw on.

The conclusion is perhaps not obvious, but essentially you have a better chance of becoming an airline pilot now than at any time in recent years. And the incentive to do so is at an all-time high.

Notes on chapter eight   There are a number of sources for job information. Some furnish free information, and some are essentially employment agencies.

Air Line Pilots Association
1625 Massachusetts Avenue, N.W.
Washington, D.C. 20036

ALPA is a well-known, well-respected organization that puts out a fine magazine and has a continuing firm grip on the general employment situation, although it does not track individual jobs.

Future Airline Pilots of America
1515 E. Tropicana Avenue
Suite 227
Las Vegas, Nevada 89101

FAPA maintains a close look at individual airline hiring and furnishes information on qualifications, recent hires, and the like. In addition, most of the larger flight schools have excellent placement programs.

Following are excerpts from the Federal Air Regulation requirements for aeronautical experience for commercial and airline pilot ratings. (There are many other transport requirements—physical, age, and so on—that are set out in FAR 61.)

(1) *Commercial Pilot*

(a) General—An applicant for a commercial pilot certificate with an airplane rating must hold a private pilot certificate with an airplane rating. If he does not hold that certificate and rating he must meet the flight experience requirements for a private pilot certificate and rating he must meet the flight experience requirements for a private pilot certificate and airplane rating and pass the applicable written and practical test prescribed in Subpart D of this Part.[sic] In addition, the applicant must hold an instrument rating (airplane), or the commercial pilot certificate that is issued is endorsed within a limitation prohibiting the carriage of passengers for hire in airplanes on cross-country flights of more than 50 nautical miles, or at night.

(b) Flight time as pilot—An applicant for a commercial pilot certificate with an airplane rating must have a total of at least 250 hours of flight time as pilot, which may include not more than 50 hours of instruction from an authorized instructor in a ground trainer acceptable to the Administrator. The total flight time as pilot must include—

(1) 100 hours in powered aircraft, including at least—

(i) 50 hours in airplanes, and

(ii) 10 hours of flight instruction and practice given by an authorized flight instructor in an airplane having a retractable landing gear, flaps and a controllable pitch propeller; and

(2) 50 hours of flight instruction given by an authorized flight instructor, including—

(i) 10 hours of instrument instruction, of which at least 5 hours must be in flight in airplanes, and

(ii) 10 hours of instruction in preparation for the commercial pilot flight test; and

(3) 100 hours of pilot in command time, including at least—

(i) 50 hours in airplanes;

(ii) 50 hours of cross-country flights, each flight with a landing at a point more than 50 nautical miles from the point of departure, including a flight with landings at three points each of which is more than 200 nautical miles from the other two points, except that those flights conducted in Hawaii may be made with landings at points which are 100 nautical miles apart; and

(iii) 5 hours of night flying including at least 10 take-offs and landings as sole manipulator of the controls.

(2) *Airline Transport Pilot*

(a) An applicant for an airline transport pilot certificate with an airplane rating must hold a commercial pilot certificate or a foreign airline transport pilot or commercial pilot license without limitations, issued by a member state of ICAO, or he must be a pilot in an Armed Force of the United States whose military experience qualifies him for a commercial pilot certificate under §61.73 of this Part.

(b) An applicant must have had

(1) At least 250 hours of flight time as pilot in command of an airline, or as copilot of an airplane performing the duties and functions of a pilot in command under the supervision of a pilot in command, or any combination thereof, at least 100 hours of which were cross-country time and 25 hours of which were night flight time; and

(2) At least 1500 hours of flight time as a pilot, including at least—

(i) 500 hours of cross-country flight time;

(ii) 100 hours of night flight time; and

(iii) 75 hours of actual or simulated instrument time, at least 50 hours of which were in actual flight.

The Spice of Flying

Aviation is more exciting than it ever was in the days of barnstormers, wing-walkers, and Tail-Spin Tommies. Despite whatever movie-engendered notions you may have of Gee Bee racers whipping around a pylon, or even of the Lone Eagle Lindbergh valiantly fighting exhaustion on his 33-hour-30-minute flight into history, today is still the most exciting time in aviation.

It's exciting in part because, while aviation has matured and become sophisticated, it has grown cool and laid back as well. The affluence of the times permits a hundred permutations of the sport that were simply beyond the reach—and the interest—of most people in aviation thirty to fifty years ago. Where once a few dozen sportsmen piloted gliders, today there are hundreds throughout the country. Where once you had to be almost blue-blooded—a member of the Long Island Country Club of the Air—to fly a fast four-passenger airplane, today thousands own and enjoy them.

Air racing— past and present

In the Golden Age of Flight (Chapter 10), when Doolittle was the dean of racing pilots and the absolute last word in high speed, performance was inevitably found at the National Air Races, and racing represented the cutting edge of aviation technology. Industry worked in its shadow, reaping the benefits of well-thought out, successful innovations, and ignoring the sometimes goofy ideas which wrapped raceplane and pilot into flaming balls at the end of the runway.

Today, just the reverse is true. Civil and military aviation technology have long since passed the point where racing is a laboratory. Instead, today's air race pilots and designers reap the rewards of industry's efforts: gleaning from modern technology the best and safest ways to make airplanes fly faster, often through the use of sophisticated computer programs. One shudders to think what Zantford "Granny" Granville, leader of the Gee Bee team, or

Jimmy Wedell, who reputedly sketched his Wedell Williams racers on the hangar floor in chalk, would say to the modern stack of computer printouts which indicate just where a line may be smoothed, or an ounce in weight reduced.

Some of the romance is gone, for the people in racing today no longer aspire to be the manufacturers of tomorrow, trying to develop one winning design which will launch them into aircraft production. Instead the air race pilots of today tend to be affluent men, whose professions permit their indulgence in an expensive, dangerous, exhilarating and usually tax-deductible hobby.

Affluent as they may be, the enormous cost of developing a racer has resulted in a rather rigid stratification of race classes.

At the top there are the big, unlimiteds, brutish World War II fighter planes, cleaned up and modified purely for speed. (There are one or two "scratch-built" unlimited racers in the works today, but their success—or even completion—is problematic.)

The modern unlimiteds tend to be largely composed of North American P-51 "Mustangs," probably the top Allied fighter of World War II and one of the two dominant aircraft in its class. The other is, of course, the Grumman Bearcat, a plane that arrived just too late to see service in the war and that was overshadowed by the advent of jet fighters by the time of the Korean Conflict. The two could hardly be more different in appearance, given the fact that they are both low-wing, all-metal, single-seat monoplanes. The Bearcat has a great round nose housing its Pratt & Whitney R-2800, tweaked and trimmed to give perhaps 2,500 horsepower; it sits high on its stalky landing gear, and has in general a pugnacious, Cagney-like air. The Mustang, on the other hand, is low and sleek and purposeful, looking always as if it wouldn't be surprised at a few Messerschmitts behind the next cloud. It is a pretty airplane from any angle, and, because it was produced in great numbers, it will dominate the racing scene as long as the unlimited class exists (Figure 9-1).

Oddly enough, a Bearcat, flown by the inimitable Darryl Greenamyer, became the world's fastest piston-engine airplane on August 16, 1969, setting a record of 483.041 mph over a 3-kilometer course. Greenamyer eclipsed Fritz Wendel's 30-year-old record of 469 mph, set in a specially modified Messerschmitt Me 109R. (It's interesting how the two men became record holders. Greenamyer did it through determination, planning, engineering skill, and a fanatical desire.

Figure 9-1.   Just as the North American P-51 Mustang was the king of fighters during World War II, so has it proved to be the king of post-war air racing. This is Scott Smith's P-51D at the Miami races.
Courtesy: Birch J. Matthews

Wendel reportedly set his because he was the junior man on the Messerschmitt test team, and the senior pilots didn't want to fly the tricky 109R!)

At the time, most people thought that Greenamyer's record would go unchallenged, for no one would spend the time and money to break what was in this age of jets a dead-end record (Figure 9-2). Not so. In 1979, a magnificently finished Rolls Royce Griffon-powered P-51, the Red Baron set a new speed record of just over 499 mph.

While most people go to air races around the country to see the unlimiteds, these planes just don't race that often. They are incredibly expensive to set up for racing, and a costly Rolls Royce engine can be turned into a heap of molten metal in seconds on the race course. Another problem is the lack of variety. As beautiful as Mustangs and Bearcats are, they get a little old after awhile, and people yearn for something different. A few "different" aircraft are around—the Hawker Sea Fury, a British counterpart to the Bearcat;

Figure 9-2a.   Darryl Greenamyer's record-breaking Conquest I, a highly modified Grumman Bearcat.
Courtesy: Smithsonian Institution

Figure 9-2b.   The magnificent RB-51, a Rolls Royce Griffon-powered, highly modified Mustang.
Courtesy: Birch J. Matthews

the famous twin-engine Lockheed P-38; and even occasionally a Bell P-63 Kingcobra (Figures 9-3, 9-4, and 9-5). None of these are really competitive with the Mustang or Bearcat. Primarily, they indulge their pilots' fancies and perhaps gain a second or third place if the "big boys" burn themselves out. In the long run, however, sheer numbers insure that the crackling roar of the Mustang's Packard Merlin engine will stay around, still luring fans to spend hours in the sun for the sake of seeing a racing start and to watch these fine old classics pulling high "G" turns around the pylons.

Stock racing

The next step down from the unlimited class is a long one, into the cockpit of another famous North American, the T-6 "Texan" (Figure 9-6). Manufactured by the thousands and used by almost every country in the free world as a trainer, the T-6 has probably trained more pilots than any other single type. It has also been used for counterinsurgency, as a FAC (Forward Air Controller) and even as an attack plane. As a result, a lot of T-6s are available at a price that

Figure 9-3.   The Hawker Sea Fury, while no match for the P-51 or Bearcat, adds color to the races.
Courtesy: Birch J. Matthews

Figure 9-4. The big Lockheed P-38 Lightning is always a crowd pleaser, even though its speed is not really competitive.
Courtesy: Birch J. Matthews

Figure 9-5. The Bell P-63 is not often a race winner, but it is loved by the crowd because it is different. Russian markings shown here are a tribute to the excellent service the plane gave under Lend Lease.
Courtesy: Birch J. Matthews

Figure 9-6.   Pat Palmer's World Champion North American T-6 racer.
Courtesy: Sandra Johnsen.

is high compared to a Cadillac but dirt cheap compared to a Mustang.

T-6 racers are essentially "stock," that is, they have not had major changes to airframe or engine that the unlimiteds are permitted. They are usually extremely well-prepared, cleaned up, waxed, and capable of lap speeds over 200 mph. With all T-6 performance closely comparable, the race is usually won by the best and most daring pilot. The T-6s have unfortunately been cursed with the worst luck of any of the racers, having been involved in two tragic mid-air collisions as well as other accidents. As a result, T-6s are—at least temporarily—not being raced.

Stock airplanes also race, but the sight of three Bonanzas circling pylons has not really set many hearts afire. Another problem is that the manufacturers hate to see their product put to a use for which it was not intended—run in a race where an accident might generate tons of unwanted publicity.

Formula One racing

Stock racing is as old as racing itself, but even in the 1930s' Golden Age, it was never as popular as races between specialized types. The closest to these "olden-day" races is found in the amazingly fast Formula One class, where tiny little monoplanes compete with only 66 square feet of wing surface (equal to a board 6 feet wide and 11 feet long!) and a stock 100-horsepower Continental engine. These little aircraft (Figure 9-7), which with their pilot weigh less than 700 pounds, hit speeds of 275 mph and more in the straight-away and rocket around pylons in knife-edged banks that sink the

Figure 9-7.   The Cassut type racer dominated Formula One racing for years. Note the small size and square slab wing.
Courtesy: Birch J. Matthews

pilots into their reclining seats. Pilot skill is paramount in these racers, even though in a race of eight airplanes the average time may vary from 190 to 200 mph. The crowd loves to see the brilliantly colored racers racking into high-G turns below the level of the pylons that mark the course.

The Formula One airplanes have recently blossomed out into a host of new configurations that add interest, if not necessarily speed, to the contest. The wing area and power constraints in no way impair the proliferation of design ideas, and in the past years there has been everything from twin-boom pushers to prone-piloted "V"-tail types. The mid-mounted slab wing had been like a uniform for Formula One, as presented by the highly successful Cassut racer type. But we now see remarkable departures from the conventional: sleek, pusher-engine types, obviously derived from intensive wind tunnel models; and a host of new wings, ranging from elliptical "mini-Spitfire" shapes to strange, almost cruciform arrangements like that of the still-developing "Wild Turkey" racer of Bob Drew (Figures 9-8 through 9-11).

Biplane racing

Even more variety can be found in another race class, which seems as much related to the Roaring Twenties as to today. The broad racing biplane class encompasses everything from well-built but

Figure 9-8.   Bob Moeller in his Formula One racer, "BOO RAY."
Courtesy: Birch J. Matthews

Figure 9-9.   Jim Miller's "Texas Gem" is one of the more unusual Formula One racers, with its pusher propeller and "Star Wars" look.
Courtesy: Dustin W. Carter

relatively slow home-built biplanes like the 170-mph Mong Sport, through genuine antique designs like the 180-mph Knight Twister (a tiny biplane with an almost notorious legend), all the way to superbly crafted special racing craft like the radical gull-wing Sorceress (which almost dominates the field). (See Figures 9-12 and 9-13.)

Like the Formula One racers, these aircraft come with inspired

Figure 9-10.   One of the most famous Formula One racers of all time, Bill Falck's "Rivets." Falck lost his life in this aircraft.
Courtesy: Dustin W. Carter

Figure 9-11.   Bob Drew's Parker JP-001 "Wild Turkey," which has an unusual wing planeform.
Courtesy: Dustin W. Carter

Figure 9-12.   The "Sorceress," a very unusual negative stagger biplane design has come almost to dominate the racing biplane class.
Courtesy: Dustin W. Carter

Figure 9-13.   Conventional in appearance, the Smith biplane racer is typical of the homebuilt racing biplanes.
Courtesy: Dustin W. Carter

paint jobs and names that range from the romantic to the censorable. All are crowd pleasers. Unlike the unlimited racers, the gaggle of biplane racers stays in sight of the crowd throughout the race, and the continuous jockeying for position is clearly visible.

The biplane racers also seem just a little more human and attainable than the bigger P-51s and Bearcats. They are fast and beautiful, but they still don't appear to be beyond the capability of the ordinary Cessna pilot. The fact is, of course, that they are extremely demanding, for they are extraordinarily sensitive to the controls; landings and takeoffs have to be made with great care. There is very little forgiveness in either Formula One or racing biplane designs.

Formula V

The cost of racer preparation has climbed in pace with everything else. In response to rising costs, the grand old man of racing, Steve Wittman, who has pioneered in most other areas in racing for more than *fifty* years, has started what may be an entire new ball game. Wittman, who learned to fly at age 20 in 1924, entered his first race in 1926 and went on to be a strong competitor in planes of his own design in almost every class of air racing. His "Buster," one of the simplest and most successful racing designs of all time, hangs in the National Air and Space Museum. The old master has now created the "Vee Witt," a Volkswagen-engine-powered racer that clearly shows the famous Wittman design heritage. As might be expected, Wittman won the very first sanctioned race for VW-powered racers, whipping the Vee Witt around the pylons at the 1927 Sturgis, Kentucky Air Races at 154 mph. Perhaps the most amazing thing about Wittman's performance is not that he won, at age 73, but that the crowd fully expected him to win!

Formula Vee racing may become one of the most important events of the future, if the energy shortage becomes as severe as some have predicted. But fuel consumption aside, the Formula Vee racers are more attainable, even more understandable than the more expensive types, and they deserve development.

Air racing of yesterday and today

What is air racing like today compared to four or five decades ago? It is a lot more scientific, with better rules and much greater concentration on safety. It doesn't seem to have the broad appeal to the public that it did in the days when the National Air Races dominated headlines for days across the country. And it has been cursed with some violent personality clashes among its leaders, which have splintered the various associations that sponsor and regulate events.

But there will always be a market for air racing. If the leadership problems can be resolved, the common problems facing the sport—fuel shortage, safety, costs—can be overcome. If they cannot, air racing will probably decline in popularity, with individual meets being organized around the country to suit the demands of a limited clientele, much as dirt track racing was conducted years ago. That would be a shame, for the sport has much to offer to both participants and public, and its worth shouldn't be submerged beneath the egos of a few of the powerful individuals involved.

Aerobatics The background of aerobatics

Ever since the Russian Nesterov looped the loop for the first time or since Lincoln Beachey did his "dive of death," the concepts of flight and aerobatics have been almost synonymous in America. Despite the barnstormers lack of airplanes that were truly aerobatic—you could force a Jenny through some maneuvers if you dived long enough to gain the necessary speed—the airshows of the late 1920s and 1930s offered a host of masterful aerobatic routines. Usually billed in as feature attractions at big air races, foreign aerobatic pilots (like Udet, Papana and others) and their American counterparts (Al Williams, Mike Murphy, Len Povey, and so on) did loops, rolls, Cuban 8s, hammerhead stalls, and ribbon cutting, all designed to keep the crowds on their feet.

After World War II a curious divergence of trends emerged. In the United States, individuals continued to fly in airshows which were often not associated with race events, in the traditional manner of Udet, Williams, and company. Foreign aerobatic pilots, on the other hand, particularly in Eastern bloc countries, began to fly much more demanding routines, which were graded rigorously by judges. In effect, the foreigners had begun an intensive, Olympic-like regimen that demanded immense precision, while the Americans persisted with air show techniques that, while skillful, did not make anything like the demand on the pilots.

There was not much awareness in America that a great transformation was taking place in aerobatics. So when Frank Price went to the international competition in Hungary in 1960, he was the sole U.S. entrant. For the next ten years, the picture did not change. American pilots began to do slightly better, for their skills were good, but they simply didn't know the rules of the game as it was being played in Europe. The first glimmering of success came in 1968, when Bob Herenden, who had carefully learned what was required, almost won the world's individual aerobatic pilot title. That seemed to be the thin edge of the wedge, for the American team went on to dominate the world championships throughout the

Figure 9-14. The "Pitts Special," a world-famous aerobatic airplane. This one belongs to Howard Serdy.
Courtesy: Tom Poberezney

1970s, including virtual clean sweeps in 1976 and 1978 (Figure 9-14).

Aerobatics for you?

What about doing aerobatics yourself? It is a great sport, but one that looks and feels entirely different when you're *doing* it from when you're watching it. From the ground, aerobatics have a ballet-like quality: you see the airplane disport itself with mathematical precision through patterns that are visually beautiful and viscerally thrilling. The view and the feel from the air is far different, and the satisfactions are not esthetic but pragmatic. Flying an airplane through a lazy loop is one thing; it is sort of fun to see the ground replace the sky momentarily and then to come out, wings level in exactly the spot you departed. Flying an Aresti* routine is a gut-wrenching, demanding, physical experience that requires intense concentration and a willingness to endure high "G" forces, rapid changes in pressure, and at least a modicum of danger.

You cannot question the fact.that becoming a master of aerobatics enhances your command of your aircraft, and, for this reason

*Aresti is a Spanish aerobatic pilot who, over the years, developed a special shorthand called "aerocryptography" for detailing the series of acrobatic maneuvers the pilot is to perform. This shorthand provides the judges with a fairly objective basis for judging an aerobatic routine.

Figure 9-15. A champion pilot and a champion aircraft—Leo Loudenslager and his Spinks Aeromaster, now called The Laser.
Courtesy: Tom Poberezny

alone, it might be worth your while. It is also a macho thing, because, if you fly, you often feel you wish you could do the things people expect you to be able to do, including a decent series of aerobatic maneuvers.

The most important thing, of course, is getting the right training in the right aircraft. Most general aviation aircraft are prohibited from doing aerobatics; they are not built to sustain the stresses that aerobatic flight places on them. Don't attempt any aerobatics in any airplane that is not licensed to perform them. And *don't attempt any aerobatics* until you have had the proper training by a certified flight instructor.

Lots of how-to books show you how to do the necessary clearing turns, what airspeeds to use, what key visual clues to look for, and what positions to push the controls to. What how-to books cannot do is induce the unusual "G" forces, provide the sudden disorientation if you lose sight of your visual key, or explain how to get out of the inverted spin you are in if you fall out of a maneuver the wrong way. *Don't read a book and try acrobatics.* It seems simple enough to say so, but some people, whose proficiency at landing a Commanche makes them think they can roll a Citabria, try to save a dollar on instruction here and there.

Owning an airplane

While racing or aerobatics may not appeal to you, you almost certainly get a letch to own your own aircraft after you fly awhile. It's a disease related to the familiar "new-car hots," a feverish condition in which you sincerely believe that it is cheaper to buy a new $10,000 automobile rather than replace four tires and a set of brakes on your old car. Actually, there are a hundred reasons to own an aircraft, of which as many as five or six make any sense at all. But you just look at the host of boats bobbing at marinas all over the country, at the hordes of hulking recreational vehicles (each equipped with rowboat, moped, and TV set) littering the highways, or, worse, at the thousand of A-frame second homes dotting half-acre "wilderness sites" around the countryside. Proprietorship and making sense are hardly ever synonymous.

Who should own an aircraft? From a practical, commercial common-sense side, only someone who uses it enough to write off the expenses and for whom it earns a rate of return on investment equal to other available investment opportunities. And that type of person accounts for perhaps 5 percent of current private owners, aside from corporations, where ownership may involve factors of prestige, convenience, or tradition that overrule economics. What about the rest?

To own or not to own

You should own an aircraft if you've thirsted to own one for years and if it will (or you think it will) make you happy. The old saw about the two happiest days of a boat owner's life are the day you buy the boat and the day you sell it applies equally well to airplanes. But let's face it: if you have an honest-to-God desire to own an airplane and if you can reasonably afford it, go ahead. You can always resell it, and, in today's market, you could conceivably even make some money on the deal.

You should own an aircraft also if the satisfaction in knowing its exact mechanical condition and flight usage is worth the expense. When you rent a plane, you trust that it has been maintained properly, that no previous renter has overstressed the airframe or engine, and that the entries in the logbooks are accurate. Most of the time, you can be reasonably secure in your faith in the operator, but still it is nothing like having your own plane, whose maintenance and flying you personally have supervised.

You should own an aircraft if it fills a psychological void that cannot be filled by a Mercedes 450 SL or a Chriscraft cruiser.

You should own an aircraft if you want an investment with real capital appreciation possibilities. Of course, this sort of ownership is specialized, for you have to seek out an antique or classic with appreciation potential. But if you are astute, you can do it.

Finally, you should own an aircraft just to own one once. After all, it isn't like marriage; it's not forever, and a plane never demands alimony. Most people, if they are careful, can buy an aircraft, fly it for a few years, and then sell it without losing much in actual dollars, if anything. In recent years inflation has raised the cost of new aircraft so drastically that used aircraft prices have been pulled along, and many a plane has actually sold for more than it cost.

Owning an aircraft also has a social effect, if you so desire. In "owner's clubs," your key to membership is the kind of aircraft you buy, just as in "Rolls Clubs" and "Jaguar Clubs" in most metropolitan areas. "Fly-ins," "dawn patrols," and other get-togethers are arranged for pilots to fly and socialize. These occasions are much like camper, van, or rec-vehicle get-togethers, except there's far less drinking, for "bottle before throttle" is a no-no. This prohibition doesn't mean that the get-togethers are absolutely dry, but drinking excessively is just considered bad form and bad judgment. The fact of the matter is that the participants are usually just "high" on flying, so the talking, the laughing, and the general goofing around are no less high-spirited for the lower alcoholic consumption.

When you decide to buy a plane you almost automatically begin to cultivate a new circle of friends at the airport, for—make no mistake—an aircraft requires at least some of the tender loving care that a sailboat does. So as you wash and polish, you'll find others doing the same, and inevitably invitations to swap rides lead to friendships.

Owning an airplane also gives you a freedom to go on vacations you'd never considered before. The country is literally spotted with resorts that are equipped with landing strips and that cater to the drop-in weekend vacationer. You'll find a lot of these far enough away to make a weekend trip in a car impractical, but just the right distance for a flight down in your own airplane.

Most of the many practical reasons for owning your own plane were covered in other chapters. Ownership can expand your business capabilities, enabling you to cover a greater territory and making better use of your time.

What are some of the "cons" of aircraft ownership? Most are financial. Unless you fly a lot, the fixed costs of ownership (depreciation, insurance, hangar fees, and so on) run hourly costs up to an unconscionable degree. A limited partnership (actually a joint-tenancy arrangement) mitigates the cost of ownership, cutting it in half with one partner up to one-tenth with nine partners. Unfortunately, all partnership ventures succeed or fail on the integrity, reliability, and mutual consideration of the people involved. Partnerships can and do work successfully, but there are often disappointments, legal entanglements, and so on in a partnership arrangement. No matter how well thought-out the articles of agreement, inconsiderate people inevitably try to hog the desirable flying days, don't do their share of the maintenance, and, worst of all, don't fly the aircraft properly.

If you don't fly 200 or more hours a year, it is almost impossible to rationalize ownership on an economic basis, especially when so many alternatives to ownership are open to you. These alternatives have their own lists of pros and cons, but they are worth examining. The pros almost always relate to financial benefits, and the cons arise from inconvenience and the potential hassles associated with others using your airplane.

The most obvious alternative to ownership for the low-use pilot is rental. It's expensive, but only apparently so. The annual interest on a $20,000 investment in an airplane can be as much as $1,800 a year, and at $30 an hour that figure translates into 60 hours of rental time right there. The practical fact of the matter is that, unless money is no object, rental is a good bet for pilots who don't fly very much.

Flying clubs are probably a better bet, for they are often well-run, paying enough of a bureaucratic price in the form of rules and regulations to insure that the members behave correctly. It's also usually easier to drop out of a flying club, if you decide that you don't like it, than it is to dissolve a partnership.

Other alternatives to ownership include leasing and purchase-and-lease-back arrangements, but they require a lot of thought and often a lawyer's advice before a decision is made.

Buying an airplane

If money is no object and if you can genuinely afford to buy a new airplane, you really have only to determine the kind of performance that you want and that your proficiency can handle. Then choose from the offerings of any of the major manufacturers. All of them are reputable, and, while some dealers are known to have better service than others, you are not going to face any major hazards when you deal with them.

Oddly enough, it's sometimes difficult to get dealers interested in you. They see a lot of Sunday shoppers, and the sales personnel are usually pursuing the corporate purchaser so assiduously that they may not take you seriously. Not to worry—simply walk out the door and go somewhere else; after you buy a new airplane, you'll want to have first-class dealer service. A dealer who isn't interested in the sale won't provide the service. You can find someone farsighted enough to be interested in you not only as a buyer of a single-engine plane today, but as the buyer of a twin-engine airplane a few years from now.

Buying a used airplane is totally different both from buying a new airplane or from buying a used car. Lots more hazards are involved, and you need to do a lot more preparation. In fact, you should enlist the aid of two friends to help you: One should be an experienced owner pilot; the other should be an experienced airframe and engine mechanic. If you don't have two friends like that, arrange to pay for someone's services to take their place; the outlay will save you money in the long run.

Don't think that a used plane dealer—company or individual— is more dishonest or more honest than a new plane dealer. It's just that you are dealing with a totally different commodity and with a much more complex business transaction. A previously owned airplane's history of use is far more vital than a used car's history, for a very obvious reason. If the used car you buy really has 156,000 miles on it, rather than the 56,000 miles shown on the odometer, an engine failure just a block down the street from the used car lot probably causes you only anger and frustration. If the used airplane you buy has had some undisclosed usage (overweight operation, student trainer use, or the like), you might find yourself running out of airspeed, altitude, and ideas all at the same time. Added to the anger and frustration may be anything from panic to horror.

Unlike used cars, however, all aircraft are supposed to have meticulously maintained logbooks that reflect their entire history. *Supposed to have.* These records are your buyer's guide to purchase, and your two friends can help you determine, from comparing the logs to the aircraft, if the records are indeed complete and accurate. Examine the logs carefully, line by line, just as you examine the aircraft carefully, nut by bolt. If the logs are reasonably accurate and your friends reasonably astute, you can determine what kind of treatment the aircraft has had, whether any accidents have occurred, and so on.

Here you will be able to check the plane's status in regard to air worthiness directives (ADs). These are mandatory instructions issued by the FAA for the correction of unsafe conditions found in aircraft over their service life. Some aircraft receive very few ADs, and others receive many. Some ADs are relatively inexpensive to comply with, but some are ruinous, causing owners to summarily scrap their planes rather than comply. It is imperative that you know what you are buying into.

Be skeptical. I had a friend who bought a lovely antique 1947 Stinson Station Wagon. He checked the oil, and found metal particles. Being prudent, he pulled the engine and shipped it across the country to a specialist who rebuilt Franklin engines. About four weeks and $2,000 later, he put the engine back on the airplane, only to find that it was a worthless melange of ill-fitting parts. The engine rebuilder was a scoundrel who had promptly gone out of business, and the $2,000 was lost forever.

In the long run, you are going to probably buy an airplane if you have the intense drive to do so—the hots. So you really ought to do the intensive planning necessary to get the best possible plane to meet your needs. I recommend that you get Timothy R.V. Foster's fine book *Aircraft Owners Handbook*. It has an immense amount of information, but, more important, it has a built-in logic system that permits you to develop and satisfy your individual requirement in a most sensible manner.

Aerial recreation

No matter how you obtain the use of a plane—buy, borrow, lease, rent, whatever—your ultimate goal is to have fun with it. Fun usually starts out as trips around the local area, savoring the pure pleasure of being "pilot in command." But this activity can quickly pall on the wife or other members of your family, who don't share the same degree of pleasure in the actual flying. So it becomes necessary to develop worthwhile recreational flights, short vacations by air.

You can work up to this gradually, as with most types of flying. Don't plan a two-week flying trip through the South Eastern portion of the United States during the summertime as your first venture. It may well be your last, for a variety of reasons. Summertime is thunderstorm time in Dixie, and few things are more frustrating than sitting on the ground at a little bitty Southern airport, waiting for those big build-ups to move on. Even if you can pick your way around them, do so only, for heaven's sake, according to standard visual flight rules. It's no fun to be bouncing up and down in 100°

temperatures, with uncertainty and anxiety showing in your face and voice. It is the quickest way to have your family sign off from flying forever.

Instead pick a destination only one or two hours of flight time away. Make sure that it has not only a good landing strip, but something fun to do for the rest of your family when you get there. If you live near Washington, D.C., for example, plan a day on the beach on the Outer Banks of North Carolina. The flight down is pleasant, the airport is adequate, and nothing is more refreshing than a dip in the brilliant blue Atlantic. Be sure no one gets too tired, and be sure you leave in plenty of time to make the flight back in daylight hours.

Next try an overnighter. Fly perhaps three or four hours to the recreation site—camping resort or whatever—and don't plan on coming back until the following afternoon. The emphasis on the vacation begins to shift from the flying part, which, whether acknowledged or not, is really your indulgence to the vacation part, which the family enjoys.

A couple of factors are at work here that should be mentioned. Weather forecasting is extremely important, and it becomes naturally more difficult to forecast for longer times. So even on short overnight trips, you have to keep constant tabs on the weather. If the forecast changes, be prepared to leave early. Don't get suckered into the trap of extending your vacation time at the risk of flying into worse weather than you really care to handle.

The next step is the extended flight: first, a week or two of touring, maybe several days of flying to get to a vacation spot across the country or in Canada or Mexico; and then several days of flying to get back. It's easy to make a persuasive case for this economically. Suppose you want to fly yourself, your wife, and two children from Atlanta to Kansas City to visit the family for a week. You'll find that you can rent a four-place airplane for about the same cost as your airline tickets, plus have the fun and experience of doing the flying yourself.

The requirement for good weather forecasting is even more important, of course, for the trip is longer. More than one vacation trip has turned into an economic disaster when a sudden change in weather forced the happy vacationers to leave the airplane at the vacation spot and return home by commercial air. Then there still remains your commercial flight back to pick up the airplane. Still, with proper planning and a little bit of luck, you can use a modern four-place, 130-knot cruise aircraft to good advantage on vacations. If you can work some legitimate business into the trip, it is so much the better, for you can deduct the appropriate amount of expenses on your income tax.

From our particular point of view, however, vacations by air are not so important for what you can do when you get there or for their economic advantage. What is important is the satisfaction you obtain from the flying and from the flyers you meet. When you drive there, literally hundreds of thousands of drivers irritate or even threaten you, driving too slow or too fast, weaving in and out, and so on. In the air you find none of this; it is not crowded in the sense highways are crowded, and courtesy prevails. The best argument for a flying vacation may well be simply that it rules out the need to drive. And you can almost be sure that you'll meet some people whom you want to stay in touch with and who will fly in to visit you in the future.

Old but not bold

An ancient saying, dating at least to 1903, says that there are old pilots and bold pilots, but no old, bold pilots. By and large that saying is true, for you *have* to be bold only in extreme circumstances—in wartime or, much more rarely, in an emergency, where boldness may turn out to be a virtue. In normal peacetime flying, however, caution and care are the rules, and there is no quicker way to lose face among your pilot peers than to do something bold where you might have done something cautious. Being bold successfully doesn't count. Just because you got away with something once doesn't mean you are smart, and it particularly doesn't mean that you'll get away with it again. Flying is best done by sensitive people who know their business well enough to be able to assess risk and take appropriate actions to minimize it.

There are a number of basic rules for longevity in flying, some obvious and others well-known. Here are just a few of them:

1. *Know thyself.* In flying, more than any other activity, you must have a clinical knowledge of your own capabilities, your relative proficiency, your physical fitness, and your mental set. If for any reason you aren't in shape for flying—don't fly.

2. *Know your equipment.* The time to start reading the owner's manual is not when the engine quits. Actually your need for the nuggets of knowledge in the manual is greatest before a flight, so that you'll be able to plan properly.

3. *Respect your intuition.* If something tells you not to make a flight, to recheck the weather, or to take one more look at the airplane, do it. Often we get subliminal clues that are not consciously perceived but that are important.

4. *Help the experts help you,* by learning as much as you can about their specialties. While you may feel you can rely implicitly on your mechanic's assurances, you can still be a big help by taking some airframe and engine courses. You can then talk more intelligently about any problems that develop. The mechanic who knows you are sharp and interested is more likely to do a better job.

    The weather office is another place where the more you know makes you easier to help. Don't be satisfied with knowing enough about weather to pass FAA exams. Learn weather as a living subject, and constantly compare what you see with what was forecast. When you begin to understand the mutual influences of air masses, geography, and seasons, you get much more out of the standard weather briefings.

5. *Never be afraid to admit to not knowing,* no matter what the subject. Never stop asking questions, even when you think you know the answers. No one—not your mechanic, the weather officer, the FAA man—minds clearing up any doubts you may have.

6. *Check your aircraft meticulously* before each and every flight, even if you are the only one flying it. Remember, you are not checking for imminent catastrophe; you are checking to prevent incipient problems. A nut that you may have checked yesterday may have vibrated loose in the last flight; if you check it again today, you'll find it needs tightening. And there is always the remote possibility of some stupid vandalism or just a careless act—a rag stuffed in the wrong spot can cause tremendous problems.

7. *Know your regulations thoroughly,* and keep current with the changes. It used to be that a general aviation pilot could fly for years and stay out of trouble just by using common sense. Not any more. The world is too complex, and you must be aware of

current regulations if you are not to be a hazard to yourself and others.

8. *Always be courteous, and never lose your temper.* Only rarely do you find "road hogs" in flying, so the stress is not comparable to driving on an expressway. Still, events can occur that tend to raise your temperature: You might be cut out of the pattern by a thoughtless student, find the taxiway blocked by someone learning how to run the checklist, or have the tower frequency jammed by some ratchet-jawed visiting pilot. Remember to relax, and always give way. It's not likely that you'll really be delayed very long or that the delay is very meaningful in the long view, anyway.

9. *Be totally honest with yourself.* If you made a bad landing, dropping the plane in, be sure to write it up even if there was no apparent damage. Similarly, if you accidently cause the engine to overspeed, find that you were operating it at an excessively lean mixture setting, or discover any other sort of incident that might prove damaging in the long run—write it up. Concealing matters like this is unethical in the extreme, for they might, in the future, carry the seeds of an accident. Once written up, they can be investigated and evaluated by a competent mechanic.

10. *Don't ever attempt anything that exceeds your capabilities.* No matter what the circumstances, no matter what the moral pressures, don't try to do anything beyond your proven ability to handle. It is amazing the blind trust that people sometimes have in a pilot's ability; they'll urge you to take risks or to fly in unfavorable conditions, simply to meet a schedule. Don't succumb to this insidious flattery; it's better to be safe in an operations office, late for an appointment, than to be fumbling through weather and wishing to God that you'd never left home.

11. *Always plan a flight so that you have several ways out—* alternate destinations, alternate routes, alternate fuel stops. Don't get suckered into a situation in which your alternatives are eliminated one by one and you are left with a situation that you can't handle.

12. *Don't be afraid to be afraid.* No one will ever criticize you for excessive caution. Fly only when it is completely comfortable to do so.

13. *Listen to your airplane.* It talks to you all the time. It may be talking with engine noise, with the way it flies, or with its performance. But it is constantly telling you its state of health, if you'll just listen.

14. *Be friendly and genuinely interested in the people who service your aircraft.* Don't taxi in, signal for service, and head for the snack bar. Stick around, check your airplane, and watch what's going on. They'll respect you for your interest and will do a better job.

15. *Ask for help when you need it.* Don't be embarrassed. If at any time you feel you're getting into difficulties—you are lost, worried about the weather, anything—get on the radio and call for help right away. The sooner you announce your trouble, the sooner someone is able to help you. Don't be shy about admitting that you are lost, that you have blundered into weather, or that you have a mechanical problem. Time is of the essence: the more time you give people to help you, the better off you are.

A hundred other rules, all of the same general nature, will be passed on to you in your reading and by your instructor. All help you get older, and none cost you a dime.

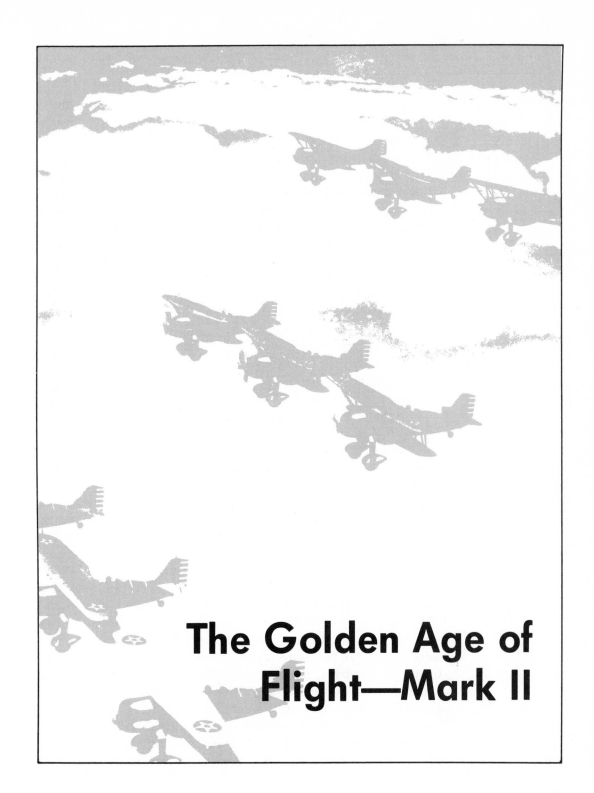

The Golden Age of
Flight—Mark II

From the stirring hours at Rheims, France, where Wilbur Wright stoically changed Europe from scoffers and scorners to impassioned disciples, through the imagined glory and real horror of two world wars, to the hassle of the middle seat on a long DC-9 flight, each and every age of flight may be called "golden." Buffs, however, generally accept the period from 1918 to 1939 as "the" Golden Age, and they have some very good reasons for doing so. During this period aircraft began to lose some of their often amateur, sometimes starkly functional lines and began to acquire a real beauty. Also during this time records were set almost weekly. Someone was always flying a little farther, higher, or faster than the man the week before, and the newspapers were quick to provide coverage.

But I don't think these are the real reasons. I think the period is considered golden simply because it was a time when great things in aviation were attainable by the seemingly ordinary man. An ordinary person, apparently just like you or me, could by imagination, effort, or an extra margin of daring superimpose his or her personality on the fabric of society and literally wrest recognition from the world. Such a person could demand to be heard.

No other period in aviation history supports such a claim. Before 1914, aviation had not yet captured everyone's imagination, and too little was known about the subject for the period to become a Golden Age. In some respects the claim was true of World War I, although the later romantic literature gave it a retrospective golden image. At the time, however, it was difficult to get into aviation; someone always wanted you to do something else, like be an infantry man, and the available slots were limited. Also, once you were in aviation, you were obliged to do not what you wished but to engage in combat; shooting and killing somewhat detracts from the golden aspects, particularly if you are not a hero at heart. (For a really incisive look at this side of wartime flying, read *Winged Victory*, a thinly fictionalized account of a British fighter squadron by V. M. Yeates.) And after 1939, things suddenly became complicated. The costs were too high, there were too many regulations, and, worst of all, aviation had become somewhat "old hat" to newspeople. The next war was the coming thing, and simply flying an airplane was not noteworthy.

But in the Golden Period from 1918 to 1939, the time was perfect for any citizen with just a few dollars to achieve fame and, much more rarely, fortune. In short, the Golden Age of aviation, like all golden ages, is based on the ascendancy of the human spirit. Never was it more obvious that an individual could prevail against obstacles, against fate, even against gravity—and achieve brilliant success in a beloved field.

From the wealth of illustrations of the Golden Age, I know of no better way to convey the flavor of the times than to give you a short insight into two background scenarios of the time. Instead of recalling the famous flights—there were so many that it would be a mere litany—or the famous battles, I want to call attention to certain events that usually pass unnoticed. Let's examine the aviation industry, starting with the incredible interrelationships of the men and companies of the Golden Age. Then let's briefly survey air racing by following the career of one small but famous company. Thus we'll see, in microcosm, what was happening behind the scenes in these fascinating years.

And for aesthetics, we'll examine a series of the most beautiful airplanes of the period, commenting briefly on their utility versus their beauty.

Finally, we'll look in at the Mark II Golden Age, the wonderful age in which we are living. It is indeed golden for the same reasons that made the 1918–1939 period golden—the primacy of the human spirit.

**The industry—
from cowshed
to cartel**

One of the most difficult things to keep in mind when we view modern space and aircraft—shuttles, SR-71s, 747s, and so on—the brief span of time between the Wright Brothers first flight and today. In the National Air and Space Museum of the Smithsonian Institution, the Apollo 11 command module *Columbia* is about 15 feet away from the Kitty Hawk Flyer in distance and only 66 years in time, from 1903 to 1969.

Many young men, born at the time when the Wrights were first experimenting with flight, came into their young manhood at the beginning of the Golden Age. Our examples are definitely not a random sample, for the related careers of these man, several of whom are alive today, illustrate the short time span involved and how intensely competitive and talented the aviation industry was from the start.

Glenn L. Martin, born in 1892, must be considered the Johnny Appleseed of the aviation industry. A brilliantly talented man, if a little odd in manner and more than a little irascible in spirit, his most remarkable talent was a faculty for picking absolutely first-rate men and giving them positions of responsibility and authority. Among his proteges were Donald Douglas, James McDonnell, Larry Bell, Dutch Kindelberger, Eric Springer, and a host of others. He rewarded them all, and he quarreled with them all. Everyone eventually left him, in dudgeons ranging from high to stratospheric, and most went on to found their own companies to compete with him.

Donald Douglas, who was eleven when the Wright Brothers flew at Kitty Hawk, was among the first to leave. He had engineered the keystone of Martin's early military success, the Glenn L. Martin bomber, and proceeded to the West Coast where he eventually founded the company that gave the world a seemingly endless series of quality aircraft. Douglas went on to create a fabulous aviation empire that exceeded Martin's in scope, one that rose in patrician fashion from one masterpiece to the next. Douglas built the first airplanes to circle the globe (the World Cruisers), the DC-3, DC-4, DC-6, DC-7, and the DC-10. On the military side, Douglas built the best of everything, from the dive bombers that won the battle of Midway to tiny attack planes. Finally, when Donald Douglas gave up the active day-to-day control of the company, it began to fall on hard times, so much so that it is now a division of the McDonnell-Douglas Aircraft Corporation.

McDonnell was also one of the irritable Glenn L. Martin's ex-proteges. Associated with some great names prior to coming to Martin (Huff-Daland and Consolidated), McDonnell stuck it out for six years between 1932 and 1938, leading the teams on some of Martin's greatest airplanes, before going to St. Louis to found his own company. After starting out by manufacturing subcontracted parts for other larger firms, he made a wartime attempt at a radical fighter, the McDonnell XP-67. Despite its weird beauty, it was a failure. A lesser man might have seen this flop and the war's end as signals to leave the aviation business. Instead, his first post-war effort, the McDonnell FH-1 Phantom, was a terrific success, the Navy's first operational carrier-based jet fighter. It led to a fabulous line of Banshees, Demons, Phantom IIs, and now the F-15 Eagle.

Another young man who emerged from this close-knit industrial Golden Age is John K. Northrop. Northrop worked first with Douglas, designing the fuel system for the famous World Cruisers, and then with Lockheed, where he designed the immortal Lockheed Vega. Not content with working for others, he started his own firm and produced the Alpha, Gamma, and others.

He was not content to build swift, streamlined aircraft; he also wanted to create economical manufacturing techniques while doing it, a trait that distinguished him from most of his colleagues. The Alpha as in metal what the Vega had been in wood—a new and better way to build. Northrop created a multi-cellular wing, manufactured with ordinary metal-working tools, that was to revolutionize the industry. The Douglas firm, with which Northrop always maintained a close working and financial relationship, used his techniques in building the DC-1, DC-2, and DC-3. Northrop went on to an unusual career of engineering innovation, to this day embracing and endorsing the idea of the flying wing.

Part of this Golden Age was the manner in which attitudes, experience, and encouragement were passed along to younger engineers. Ed Heineman, creator of a number of classic designs, had the benefit of working with both Douglas and Northrop. He borrowed a saying from the famous William Stout, promoter for the Ford Tri-motor: "Simplicate and add Lightness." He is famous for his clever, economic engineering methods. One of his most famous efforts, the McDonnell Douglas A-4 Skyhawk, went into production in 1952 and stayed there for 26 years.

Heineman did not lend his name to a manufacturing company, nor did, mercifully, Dutch Kindleberger, although the latter was a prime mover in the founding of what became North American Aviation. Kindleberger had worked for both Martin and Douglas. So when he began the great firm that built the P-51 Mustang, the B-25 Mitchell, and the F-86 Sabre, among many others, he began with a background in engineering and manufacturing that virtually guaranteed success.

The litany of names could go on and on, but the point is that the original manufacturing companies—Martin, Curtiss, Consolidated, and others—were like forges for young design genuises. Like raw ores, these talented people were drawn into the refining furnaces, where the shared knowledge, techniques, inspirations, and ambitions spilled out as finished metal. Often with the most minimal investment capital, these entrepreneurs set up the aviation industry almost as we know it today.

To really appreciate the achievements of these entreprenurial daredevils, we must examine their success against the background of the times and in terms of the numbers who failed. The Golden Age was characterized by a brief period of prosperity immediately after the war, followed by a longer recession that turned into the runaway boom of the late 1920s. The cataclysmic depression followed, lasting from 1929 until World War II. For each Martin or Douglas company that survived these dismal years, when aircraft orders were counted in ones and twos or at most in tens and twenties, dozens of others faltered and finally withered away. The list is almost endless: from the Aerial Service Corporation through Zenith; from tiny, under-financed, unknown firms like Dycer to huge, seemingly well-financed giants like Berliner-Joyce, Atlantic, and so on. The difference between success and failure, of course, was in the talent of the men running the businesses, and here the giants of the Golden Age gained their real luster.

We've examined just one cluster of talent. There were similar clusters, elsewhere. McCook Field, the predecessor of both Wright-Patterson and Edward Air Force Bases, was another Golden Age hothouse of designers and engineers who came together, interacted, competed, and then went on to industry. From McCook Field came such giants as Virginius Clark, who developed both the Clark Y airfoil and the Duramold process, with which Howard Hughes' gigantic flying boat was built. Reuben Fleet founded Consolidated Aircraft and ran it with iron discipline until he retired. Don Berlin designed the unforgettable Curtiss P-40 and many other aircraft. I. M. Laddon, Fleet's strong right arm, designed the PBY, B-36, and others. The list could go on and on.

There is a point to all this name-dropping, and that is the relative ease with which talented engineers could express themselves. Companies, even governmental agencies, were small enough that any engineer fortunate enough to be employed was also fortunate enough to be given important work to do.

The situation today is vastly different in major corporations.

Instead of a few bright-eyed young men, bending metal and consulting with the blue-collar workers as well as with the test pilots, elaborate, faceless bureaucracies shield any genius behind rows and rows of drafting tables. Imagine, if you will, the exciting, wild, sometimes profanity-filled discussions that must have taken place among Glenn Martin, Larry Bell, Don Douglas, and others as the first Glenn Martin Bomber was taking shape in Cleveland in 1918. Or picture those among Northrop, Kindelberger, and Douglas when the World Cruisers were being built, or those among Fleet, Clark, and Laddon as the PBY Catalina was going together.

Today a new engineer would be lucky even to see the production line, much less have a vital part in making it work. Far from having a chance to argue face-to-face with the boss, modern engineers work a drafting board, their slide rules replaced by a Japanese calculator. Instead of being asked to design, say, a fuel system, they're often required to figure out how to reduce the weight of a cotter pin from 5 to 4 grams. The work is important, of course, but how do they make their mark today? Can you imagine their leaving, after four or five years of cotter pin weight reduction work, saying, "I'm going to found my own aircraft company?" In today's world they must be organization-oriented first *and* politicians, as well as engineers.

This aspect of the Golden Age was important but often overlooked—the brilliant outpouring of talent that literally thrust America into the forefront of aviation. The human climate that permitted such a flow no longer exists in industry, but it exists elsewhere, as we shall see.

Air racing— crown jewel of the Golden Age

The thrusting forward of brilliance against adversity was repeated in microcosm in the racing world. Aircraft were set to racing each other almost as soon as we were capable of getting two in the air at the same time. Few things were more natural to Americans than air racing, for it combined in one magnificent sport many national loves. Americans soon discovered that they loved airplanes per se, for their embodiment of speed, freedom, and that essential spice, danger. Finally, Americans love carnivals and fairs, and air racing seemed to combine all these loves into one lusty, spectacular sport that reached its peak during the Golden Age.

Racing has long been an important component of flight. But it didn't assume a serious developmental role until the years just after the first world war, when the Schneider and Pulitzer races turned into research and development arenas for both engines and fighter aircraft. The immediate benefits of racing to military aviation were enormous. The Pulitzer races saw the development of the historic line of Curtiss, Wright, and Verville types, while the Schneider races would be immortal if they had developed only the line of Supermarine seaplanes, which led ultimately to Reginald Mitchell's imcomparable Spitfire.

Several factors altered the early military dominance of air racing. In the first place, the depression reduced military spending to the point that the increasing costs of developing and testing a racer could not be explained to the Congresses and Parliaments of the world. In the second place, there grew an increasing difference between the requirements of a combat aircraft—to carry oxygen, guns, and fuel and to execute high "G" maneuvers—and the one requirement of a racer, which was pure speed.

As a result, the racing scene hatched a development previously considered impossible: a civil aircraft with performance higher than contemporary military fighters. In 1929 Doug Davis flew his Travel Air R "Mystery Ship" to victory in the National Air Races. Bank-rolled by Walter Beech and his Travel Air Company and designed by Herb Rawdon and Walter Burnham, the low-wing, sleekly cowled and spatted aircraft averaged just under 195 mph to win the main event. It also unleashed a veritable riot among hungry, starved-for-success civil race plane builders.

All across the country, smart eager young men—some pilots, some designers, some both—looked at the Mystery Ship and said, "If Beech can do it, so can I." So for 1930 a host of new planes competed, planes whose names would soon become synonymous with racing. There was a Laird Solution (to the Travel Air "Mystery," of course), a Howard "Pete" (one of the first of Benny Howard's DGAs, Damned Good Airplanes), and others. Charles "Speed" Holman won the race in the Solution at 201.9 mph, and again all over the country eager young pilots cried, "Why not me?"

Among those asking this burning question was a band of brothers ably led by young Zantford B. "Granny" Granville of Springfield, Massachusetts. Granny and his four brothers, Mark, Ed, Tom, and Bob, had a struggling aircraft factory going and in the course of three hectic years had produced about twenty airplanes. These were the Granville brothers, and their products were of course the memorable Gee Bees. Although the Granvilles had been building nice, attractive sport planes, they weren't making any money. The depression had them, as it had most manufacturers, by the throat. Their monoplane sportsters had been fast, and in fact they had been used in some minor race events. So it seemed logical to enter the air racing arena on a larger scale. The Granvilles were the Golden Age defined: no money, lots of skill, great opportunity, and high risk. They were absolutely devoid of money, but they had the immense good will of the people of Springfield, along with unending energy.

Granny was a true leader. He could push his team to work straight through for yet another 48 hours, and keep them laughing with jokes and slight gags while doing it. He had a beguiling way of threading a long cable through the coat sleeves of an unsuspecting visitor, keeping him occupied with an amusing flow of chatter, until the victim was almost ensnarled—not very funny on paper, but hilarious at two o'clock in the morning on the day that you are supposed to roll out your world-beating racer. The elder Granville had a natural eye for design and a good intuition for aerodynamics; he was also a superb pilot as well as a skilled craftsman.

And Granville had a fine team behind him. His brother Mark was also a fine pilot and a magnificent welder, an important talent in those days of steel tube fuselages. Tom was a great woodworker, able to translate spruce timbers and plywood sheets into super-streamlined shapes. Brother Ed was another fine welder and a great metalworker besides; he was also an accomplished pilot. Bob, who was the last of the Granville brothers and who lived to see his famous family brought back into the spotlight once again, was also a craftsman, but he took care of the business end of things, which consisted primarily of placating bill collectors. Granny, smart enough to realize that he needed to reinforce his native judgment with the services of a trained engineer, hired Bob Hall, also a pilot and a fine engineer, to validate his intuitive ideas.

Not until two months before the National Air Races were scheduled to begin was sufficient capital gathered to build a racer. Working night and day, the Granville brothers turned out the squat, powerful-looking Gee Bee Model Z, the City of Springfield (Figure 10-1).

Figure 10-1.   Lowell Bayles and the Granville Brothers' most successful G ee Bee racer, the "City of Springfield." Bayles won the Thompson Trophy in 1931 in this aircraft, then lost his life in it while attempting to set the world's land speed record.
Courtesy: Peter M. Bowers

This yellow-and-black racer, far different in appearance from any previous contestant, made its first flight only one week before the air races were to begin. Arriving from Springfield, the Gee Bee created a sensation, and wags said that it looked like a Travel Air Mystery Ship that had flown into the wall. The Model Z was immensely successful, winning every event it entered, including the prestigious Thompson Trophy Race, and coming very close to setting a world's absolute landing speed record. Besides winning the Thompson, Lowell Bayles also won the Greve Trophy race and the Shell Speed Dash, while Bob Hall also won a less competitive race.

The Granvilles and their backers in Springfield were ecstatic. Here was the true realization of the American dream. Five brothers had put together a record-setting racer, winning against the best that America—and by inference, the world—had to offer. In some respects this undiluted satisfaction was the high point of the Granville brothers' career. Joy was as yet unmarred by tragedy.

Unfortunately, it was not long before tragedy became an essential, almost quintessential, part of the Gee Bee story. Not content with the air race successes, the Granville brothers hung an even larger engine and propeller on the Model Z, and Lowell Bayles made three attempts on the world land plane speed record. The attempts failed for various technical reasons, including the malfunction of timers.

Then on December 5, 1931, he made the fourth attempt. Some say a gas cap came off, striking the canopy and either startling or incapacitating Bayles. For still unexplained reasons, Bayles apparently made a control movement that induced excessively high "G" forces. A wing snapped off, and the plane plunged into the ground, killing the pilot.

Undaunted, the Granvilles took all their resources to build not one but two aircraft for the 1932 racing season, which they knew would be a head-on competition with their arch rival, Jimmy Wedell's Wedell Williams. Jimmy Wedell had a lot in common with Granny Granville in terms of background, education, methodology, and, curiously enough, even physical appearance. He was different in one important respect, however: He had the financial backing of millionaire Henry Williams. Where Granny had to beg, borrow, and scheme to keep creditors from the door, Wedell had ample funds.

Both Granny and Wedell were to die in nonrace-related aircraft accidents within six months of each other in 1934.

The 1932 Gee Bees were in many ways the absolute zenith of the Golden Age, and they have been maligned over the years as pilot killers, "shady ladies of the skies," death ships, and so on. If one looks only at their racing records, the allegations seem true. But if you look at them from another perspective, from the Granville brothers' viewpoint in that early-1930 time frame, a different picture emerges.

Granny had an intuitive theory about streamlining, which differed vastly from contemporary practice and which he developed fully in his 1932 racers. He felt that you could afford the relatively large frontal area inevitably associated with a powerful radial engine, if the widest part of the airplane was a point about a third of the way from the front of the fuselage, not the cowling around the engine. The thickest part was therefore just about in the same place as the main spar of the wing span. This resulted in a teardrop shape, almost the reverse of modern area rule technology. In addition, Granny felt that the fuselage length should be as short as possible. This theory was strictly intuition on Granny's part, and he hired a brilliant young engineer named Howell "Pete" Miller to validate the concept for him. To Granny's immense gratification, Miller's extensive wind tunnel tests proved his theory correct.

Despite the 1931 successes, the Granvilles had relatively little money, and they built their two 1932 racers for about $6,000 each. They were able to do so because manufacturers were anxious to loan components—engines, propellers, tires, and other parts—for the privilege of advertising their wares. Other manufacturers would donate fabric, dope, and other elements for the right to have their names inscribed prominently on the finished racers.

The Granvilles were aiming for a clean sweep of the big prizes of the 1932 air races: first in the Bendix and Thompson races, plus as many other firsts and seconds as they could amass. To accomplish this goal, they designed two essentially identical aircraft, which differed only in the engine used and the amount of fuel load planned. The first, the R-1, was designed for the closed-course Thompson Race and was powered by an uprated Pratt & Whitney engine of 800 horsepower, with which they expected a top speed of 298 mph. The second plane, the R-2, was intended primarily for the long-distance Bendix Race, where range was almost as important as speed, so it was fitted with a smaller, more fuel-economic 550-hp engine. The R-2 carried 302 gallons of gas, compared to the R-1's 160. Both airplanes were beautifully finished, with scientifically tested wing and empennage fillets, which added to their speed. The typical Gee Bee red-and-white scalloped paint job was enhanced with a rolling pair of dice insignia which naturally came up 7 and 11.

Then the combination of two accidents, each unfortunate in itself, turned out to be the greatest bit of luck the Granvilles ever had. Russell Boardman, an experienced pilot and heavy financial backer of the Granville efforts, had been intending to fly the R-1 in the Thompson. He injured himself in a crash and was unable to fly. Almost simultaneously, Jimmy Doolittle, testing an improved version of the winner of the prior year's Thompson Race, was forced to crash land. Doolittle no longer had a plane, and the Granvilles no longer had a pilot. The solution was obvious, and Doolittle came to Springfield. Doolittle was probably the best and most experienced high-speed test pilot in the country, and that was exactly what was needed to get maximum performance from the Gee Bee racer and survive. He came to Springfield, examined the R-1, got in, and instead of test hopping it, flew it directly to Cleveland for the air races.

A master pilot, Doolittle perceived that the way to victory was to fly a conservative race, circling the pylons high and wide, and then blasting ahead in the straightaways. He finished first with a record-breaking 252 mph, a mark that would last for four years before being topped (Figure 10-2).

Doolittle also set a new world's land speed record in another set of trials, flying the R-1 at 296 mph, with a one-way speed of 309 mph. He very wisely retired from racing at this point, observing

Figure 10-2. The famous Jimmie Doolittle flying the G ee Bee R-1. He was the only pilot to really "tame" the powerful racers, and he was wise enough to stop racing while he was still ahead of the game.
Courtesy: Peter M. Bowers

that very few race pilots lived to a ripe old age. When in later years he was asked how he flew the Gee Bee, he would always reply with his famous grin, "Very carefully."

The other Gee Bee entry, the R-2, didn't fare as well. Lee Gehlbach had an oil leak and cowling trouble and couldn't finish the Bendix. He managed to place only fifth in the Thompson, a sore disappointment.

From this point on, the Golden Age became tarnished for the Granvilles. Neither the R-1 or R-2 ever won another race. Russ Boardman was killed in the R-1 in 1933, and the pilot of the R-2 was so shaken by the event that he withdrew from the race. Granny himself was killed in 1934, and minor accidents kept the remaining Gee Bee racer, a hybrid of the R-1 and R-2, from racing. It was ultimately destroyed in 1935 when an inexperienced flyer, who had modified it substantially, wrapped it and himself into a ball off the end of the runway at Los Angeles at the start of the Bendix Race.

A final Gee Bee racer, the Q.E.D. for Quod Erat Demonstrandum (it is proved), never lived up to its possibilities and never finished a race in which it was entered. It did have one brief moment of glory when Captain Francesco de Sarabia set a Mexico-City-to-New-York record in it. A few days later, after being feted as a hero in New York and Washington, D.C., Serabia was taking off from Bolling Field. A rag was sucked into his carburetor, and the engine quit. The Q.E.D. plunged into the Potomac, and Serabia drowned. Curiously, the Q.E.D. is the only Gee Bee racer to survive; it was dredged from the river and sent back to Mexico where the Serabia family had it restored. It is on display in Cuidad Lerdo.

Were the Gee Bees cursed? Were they really winged death traps? Or were they simply appropriate ornaments that lent the Golden Age its luster of danger and death? In actual fact, they represent the very best of the Golden Age and the very worst. On the positive side they were extremely advanced examples of engine and airframe technology, and they were expressions of a native American genius. On the negative side, many aspects of the Golden Age are revealed not by the Gee Bees themselves, but in the environment in which they were flown. The testing of air racers was terribly primitive. Just imagine, the fastest plane in the world was rolled out only two weeks in advance of the day it was required to race. There was literally no time for testing.

If the race rules of the time had, for example, required a 6-month, 50-hour test program for each of the racers, the Gee Bees could have been refined to the point where it took less than a giant like Jimmy Doolittle to fly them correctly. Similarly, racing rules didn't define pilot qualifications very well, and many lives were lost needlessly.

Just as the Gee Bees plumbed both the heights and the depths of the Golden Age, so can parallel examples be found not only in racing, but in military aircraft, light planes, transports, and so on. And perhaps the bad points as much as the good points humanize the period.

Figures 10-3 through 10-7 give us a look beyond racing and industry at some of the aircraft that really brought the title of "Golden Age" into prominence. Photos like these could easily lead us to end on a note of bitter sweet nostalgia, to sigh for the long-gone days of the Golden Age, and to bemoan the fact that bureaucracy, taxes, legislation, inflation, and the fuel shortage make the Golden Age impossible to achieve again.

The new golden age

Curiously, these contemporary curses have had just the reverse effect and have in a very real way created a climate that has permitted the coming of a second Golden Age, which in many ways is far superior to the first. In actual practice the bureaucracy of general and commercial aviation is so great and complex that it

Figure 10-3.

The Curtiss JN-4—The famous Jenny was a transition plane from the World War I era, and it gave many of the pilots and designers of the Golden Age their first practical experience of flight.
Courtesy: Smithsonian Institution

Figure 10-4.   **American Eagle**—Almost prototypical of the biplanes of the period, this three-place aircraft was powered by a 90-hp OX-5 engine that hurtled it along at a 90-mph speed. Note the burnished cowling, almost **de rigueur** after the Lindbergh flight. The man behind this airplane, Ed Porterfield, would contribute much to the Golden Age. Courtesy: Smithsonian Institution

Figure 10-5.   **Waco Cabin**—Just how far and how fast the biplane came is shown in this Waco, capable of seating four with a maximum speed of about 140 mph.
Courtesy: Smithsonian Institution

Figure 10-6.   **Beech Staggerwing**—The Learjet of its day, the Beech D-17 was an incredible performer, one that has a loyal clientele and even a museum dedicated to it today. With its unique appearance, retractable landing gear, and high speed, the Staggerwing Beech earned an immortal place in history.

simply cannot be extended to the Golden Age of which we speak, the age of the Experimental Aircraft Association, and of home-built airplanes. Inflation has driven the price of conventionally manufactured aircraft up to the point where they are beyond the means of the ordinary man, who now, however, has the option of turning to the home-built field.

There has been a revolution, a rebellion, a turning away from the mass-manufactured $40,000 "spam Cans" from Wichita, to a vast new market that only a few believe existed. The Experimental Aircraft Association has grown from a small club in one man's cellar in 1953 to a huge international organization with more than 600 chapters and 62,000 members. It is well-organized and aggressive, and it has irresistably demonstrated not only that this is a new

Figure 10-7.   **Curtiss P-6E**—Perhaps the most photogenic of all biplane fighters of the period, the **Curtiss Hawk,** with its flashy paint job, starred at every air show of the 1930s. Its actual performance, however, was a little inferior to most of the other biplane fighters of the time.

Golden Age but that the old Golden Age can live on in rebuilt antique aircraft.

Founded by Paul Poberezny, who is still Chairman and mainspring, the EAA is a successful demonstration that all of the old American virtues of ingenuity, craftsmanship, prudence, and comradeship are alive and well and only waiting for a chance to boil to the surface. Besides its extensive membership and very active local, the EAA puts out a great magazine. *Sport Aviation* gives advice and courses on how to build airplanes, publishes innumerable manuals on the subject, has an outstanding museum of experimental types, and an annual fly-in at Oshkosh, Wisconsin, which is truly one of the most remarkable festivals of the Western

World. As many as 12,000 aircraft fly into Steve Wittman Field, with thousands of them home-built by their owners. Held in an atmosphere of good will and camaraderie, the Oshkosh Fly-In has become a Mecca for American pilots. The best think about EAA, of course, is the unbounded enthusiasm of its thousands of members, who are anxious to help each other, to show off their wares, to teach, to learn, and to recruit.

One particularly delightful aspect of this phenomenon is its totally democratic aspects. It does not matter a whit if you are a governor of a state, a brain surgeon, a filling station attendant, or a student. What *does* matter is your involvement in the movement, your commitment to flying, and the relative success you have had in attaining your own goals in terms of building and flying the airplane you yourself want.

The raison d'etre of the EAA is the home-built aircraft, and there has been an incredible expansion from the first prize winning *Mechanic's Illustrated* parasol monoplane that Poberezny built in the early 1950s to the unlimited number of aircraft types available for kit building today. You can build everything from a hang glider

Figure 10-8. The Wittman Tailwind is a synthesis of two golden ages. Steve Wittman has been a designer and a race pilot for more than 50 years, and he is still doing both. The Tailwind first appeared in 1950, as his special, fast, personal airplane, and it has since been built by many others in many versions. This one is Steve's latest, powered by an Oldsmobile V-8 automobile engine.

or sailplane to a racer to a three-quarter-scale World War II fighter, from plans and kits that have been carefully reviewed for their ease of building and safety.

Second in the EAA program is the restoration of antiques, that joyful experience of finding a basket case stored in an old barn and carefully and lovingly restoring it to its original state.

Then there are the War Birds owners. This is indeed a group apart, wealthy men for the most part who wish to recapture the nostalgia of World War II by flying real aircraft from the period, everything from T-6 trainers to P-51 Mustangs to Messerschmitts, Spitfires, and yes, even B-29s.

The EAA has room for all the various subgroups—powered hang gliders, flying boats, and so on.

Besides the patterns of democracy and strong attitude of self-help among the members, the EAA is characterized by other qualities. First and foremost is their concern for safety. A series of accidents resulting from poor judgment or poor craftsmanship on the part of EAA members could spell the end of the organization. During the late 1920s and early 1930s there was a smaller, similar, but far less structured flowering of home-built aircraft. There were no inspections and certainly no EAA from which to obtain help. As a result a rash of accidents precipitated legislation ending the boom. EAA doesn't want this to happen, and it takes effective measures to see that it does not.

Another EAA trademark is the almost unbelievable craftsmanship that characterizes the work of the builders. It is a mind-boggling experience to walk through the rows and rows of home-built and antique aircraft at Oshkosh and to see the care lavished on each one. Untold hours of sanding, polishing, and waxing are evident, as well as immeasurable pride in the faces of the owners. As evidence of this, let's look at a representative sample of their work, and see if you won't agree that this, too, is a Golden Age (Figures 10-8 through 10-28).

It is easy to sweep all nostalgia aside, clean out the garage, and start ordering parts when aircraft like this are available at prices that are very attractive compared to a new foreign car.

Figure 10-9. Taylor's Tinker Toy—something different—has only average performance but a unique appearance among homebuilts.

Figure 10-10. Hirondelle means swallow, and it is shown to illustrate the beauty that can be obtained with conventional all-wood construction. Powered by a Lycoming 108-hp engine, the Hirondelle has a top speed of 140 mph and a cruise of 135.

Figure 10-11. All-wood construction does not necessarily mean a tame, unsophisticated aircraft. This is Geoffrey Siers' Barracuda. Siers, a former RAF pilot, wanted an easy-to-build plane with good looks, high performance, and low cost.

Figure 10-12. Dr. S. F. Brokaw wanted approximately the same thing as Siers, except that he expressed it as a "simulated Bearcat." Brokaw, a dentist and former Navy pilot, worked in metal, and it took him six years, 7,000 hours, and many thousands of dollars to achieve his dream. It's worth it, for the BJ-250 is a beautiful, unique airplane with a top speed of 300 mph.

Figure 10-13. Some people want something even more unusual than a homebuilt aircraft, so they turn to rotor craft. This Columbo Super Scorpion is an amazing example of a nonbuilder, nonhelicopter pilot choosing a project and having the time and talent to turn it into a EAA Grand Champion prize winner.

Figure 10-14.   Burt Rutan is almost a cult figure among home-builders, for he has turned out an apparently unending series of unorthodox but immensely successful home-builts. This, the Varieze, is being built in large numbers all across the country, despite its unusual configuration and advanced fibreglass construction. Rutan is a name to remember; he will be an important figure in aviation for years to come, and not only in the field of home-builts.

Figure 10-15.   Sometimes home-builders strive for the lightest or the smallest or the simplest. The Raz-mut is an effort in the direction of the minimum airplane. Powered by a 1,700-cc Volkswagen engine, the Raz-mut is essentially a winged gyroplane.

Figure 10-16.   On the other hand, some people want conventional-looking aircraft with unconventional structure. This REP-2 has an aluminum tubular spar wing, built up with styrofoam and covered over with fibreglass. For many EAA people, there is as much fun in building as in flying.

Figure 10-17.   Other home-builders take a conventional design with conventional structure and then build it better than anyone else. This is the 1977 Grand Champion Stolp Starduster Too, built by Roger Rourke. He has a total of 9 years and 8,000 hours of labor in the airplane, of which 2,000 hours alone are sanding. The result, a 153-mph, fully acrobatic, prize-winning, head-turning airplane.

Figure 10-18.   Sometimes the whole top brass of the EAA gets wrapped up in a project, like Lindbergh's fiftieth anniversary celebration, so they built a reproduction of Spirit of St. Louis. They flew it not across the Atlantic (although I bet the idea was toyed with) but instead on a 102-town, 48-state tour, in which it was amazingly well received.

Figure 10-19.   The ultimate aim of the antique aircraft lover is to find not only an old classic in a barn but, wherever possible, a one-of-a-kind classic. That is exactly what Forest Lovely did with this Kari-Keen Sioux Coupe, the 1977 EAA Grand Champion.

Figure 10-20. Warbirds are a special breed, involving higher levels of both skill and money. This XP-51 was restored by EAA and is flown at their fly-ins, usually by Paul Poberezney himself.

Figure 10-21. The T-6 is another popular warbird, for it is relatively inexpensive and relatively cheap to run—compared to a P-51. This is John Harrison's Grand Champion Warbird, an AT-6A.

Figure 10-22. This is WAR! At least it is a War Aircraft Replica Focke Wulfe FW 190, a VW-powered, 20-foot wing span miniature of the famous German fighter. Construction is unorthodox, with foam and dynel construction permitting the complex curves to be made readily.

Figure 10-23. But the big favorites are warbirds like the Curtiss P-40,

Figure 10-24.   Hawker Sea Fury and Grumman Wildcat.

Figure 10-25.   Messerschmitt BF 109 (actually a Merlin-engined Spanish-built air-craft).

Figure 10-26.   A Douglas Skyraider, better known as the Spad.

Figure 10-27.   The ever popular P-38 Lightning.

Figure 10-28.   And perhaps the penultimate home-built, the Gossamer Condor.

But you don't have to build you own airplane, or race, or do aerobatics to become a part of this new Golden Age. Instead, take it one step at a time, ease in, and take a little trip out to your favorite small airport. Perhaps you'll find that it is indeed now time for you to fly.

Index

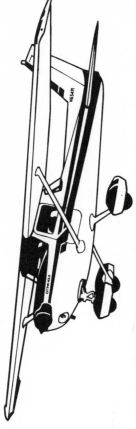

Take Off with a
Cessna Pilot Center
Discovery Flight

Cessna PILOT CENTER

Discover Flying

This coupon entitles you to a special rate for a Cessna Pilot Center Discovery Flight. You'll receive a preflight briefing, a Discovery Flight during which you'll actually fly the airplane under the direction of a Certified Flight Instructor, and a special after-the-flight evaluation.

It's Cessna's way of introducing you to the most popular flight training program in the world, developed by the world's leader in General Aviation. The Cessna Pilot Center system brings flight training down to its simplest form, and makes it easy for everyone to learn to fly.

Since individual Cessna Pilot Centers establish their own individual procedures for Discovery Flights, check in advance with your local Center [see the Yellow Pages]. Bring this coupon or this book with you. If you can't locate a Cessna Pilot Center, write to Cessna, P.O. Box 1521, Wichita, Kansas 67201 for a complete directory.